ESSENTIALS OF INTELLECTUAL PROPERTY FOR THE PARALEGAL

by
Christian R. Andersen

With introduction and contributions by
Janis M. Manning, Esq.

Copyright 1998

Pearson Publications Company
Dallas, Texas

ISBN 0-929563-44-1

Essentials of Intellectual Property for the Paralegal is designed as a textbook for classroom use. The book and the forms and tables contained herein are intended only for education and informational purposes.

**See website
http://home1.gte.net/chrisand/**

DEDICATION

This book is dedicated to the people who made my career in the field of intellectual property possible and fulfilling, namely:

➢ my grandmother Nathalie Theresa Andersen, who first taught me the value of a trade name through her store,

➢ attorneys Molly Buck Richard and Janis M. Manning, who gave me support and guidance, and most important,

➢ my parents, Christian A. Andersen and Betty Jean Andersen, who have provided constant love, support and inspiration.

Christian R. Anderson

ACKNOWLEDGMENTS

In addition to the author and contributors, I want to thank the many other individuals who have added to the excellence of the final product:

Professors Ann Cohen of Amherst, MA, and Roy S. Gordet of San Francisco, CA; Andy Hassell, Esq., Dallas, TX, and Mark J. Patterson, Esq., of Nashville, TN; as well as Carolyn Bullard, Linda Furlet, Sherry Hartman, and Frances Whiteside, whose energy and precision helped make this book the premier paralegal textbook on intellectual property.

Enika Pearson Schulze
Publisher

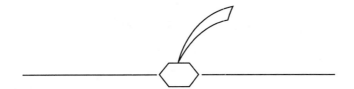

TABLE OF CONTENTS

INTRODUCTION

By Janis M. Manning, Esq.

The field of intellectual property law has experienced tremendous growth in recent years due to the ever increasing importance of businesses competing in the global marketplace. This competition has fostered heightened awareness of the value of intellectual property assets and an interest in the protection of such assets internationally. The concept of intellectual property is also referred to as "industrial property" and includes such assets as patents, trademarks, and copyrights.

Patents

A **patent** is a right granted by the government of a country that excludes other parties from making, using, or selling an invention. In order to be patentable in the United States as a **utility patent**, an invention must be a new and useful process, machine, article of manufacture, or composition of matter. For example, a mechanical or electrical process, a machine such as a boat engine, an article of manufacture such as a hand tool, and chemical compositions such as plastic are patentable. A **design patent** covers original and ornamental designs for an article of manufacture.

Inventions are patented for a limited period of time in each country. There is no such thing as an "international" patent that protects an invention around the world. Once a patent expires, the invention may be freely used by anyone in that country.

Trademarks

A **trademark** is any word, name, symbol, device, or any combination thereof that is used by a manufacturer or merchant to identify its products or services and to distinguish them from the products or services of others. For example, the mark EXXON® identifies the oil products and services of Exxon Corporation and distinguishes them from the MOBIL® oil products and gas station services of the Mobil Oil Company.

In the United States, trademark rights are based on use in the marketplace and not on registration. While registration of a trademark provides the owner with important advantages and benefits, registration is not a prerequisite to trademark rights. Rights in the trademark will last as long as the trademark is used in the marketplace.

In many foreign countries, however, rights in a trademark are granted to the first party to register the trademark, irrespective of whether the trademark has been used. As with patents, there is no such thing as an international registration that protects a trademark globally. For the most part, separate trademark applications must be filed in each country. There are, however, multinational treaties and arrangements that provide for the registration of a trademark in numerous countries, such as the filing of a Benelux application covering Belgium, Luxembourg and the Netherlands. Another example is the filing of a European Community trademark application covering all 15 countries of the European Union.

Copyright

Copyright protects the particular *expression* of an idea that is created and fixed in a tangible form, such as writing or an audiovisual work. Copyrightable works cover the following: categories:

> ➤ literary works
> ➤ musical works, including accompanying words
> ➤ dramatic works, including accompanying music, pantomimes and choreographic works
> ➤ pictorial, graphic and sculptural works
> ➤ motion pictures and other audiovisual works
> ➤ sound recordings
> ➤ architectural works.

Copyright protection does not extend to any idea, procedure, process, system, method of operation, concept, principle, or discovery. It is not the general idea but, rather, the specific expression of an idea, that is protectable under copyright law.

A copyright is created the moment a copyrightable work is created and fixed in a tangible form. For example, the moment I write down an original poem on a piece of paper, I have a copyright in that poem. The copyright is owned by the author who created the work. There is no requirement for registration in order to create a copyright in a work. There are, however, benefits to registering a copyright. Copyright protection is limited in duration. Once the term expires, the work is released into the public domain and may be used by anyone.

A copyright provides the owner with the exclusive right to reproduce the work, to prepare derivative works based on the work, to distribute copies of the work, and to perform and display the work publicly.

Numerous international treaties define the protection afforded a copyright in the various member countries that do not include registration as a prerequisite for protection. In fact, in many foreign countries, there is no procedure for even registering a copyright.

Other Intellectual Property Rights

Other intellectual property rights consist of trade secrets, publicity rights, privacy rights, semiconductor chip protection, and plant variety protection.

The Role of the Paralegal

There are employment opportunities for intellectual property paralegals in corporations, in large general practice law firms having an intellectual property practice group, or in law firms that specialize in intellectual property law. The practice of intellectual property law is dynamic, because it focuses on the marketplace activities of businesses that are constantly introducing new products and services, thereby creating new intellectual property rights to be protected. A new product or service may involve the creation of rights protectable under the patent, trademark, and copyright laws, and may also involve other areas of intellectual property.

A paralegal is a valuable resource to an intellectual property attorney. Many of the tasks involved in securing protection for patents, trademarks, and copyrights discussed in this book are well suited to the paralegal, subject to the attorney's review. For example, a paralegal will search to determine whether a proposed trademark is available for use and registration or determine who is the record owner of a patent or a trademark or copyright registration.

Other appropriate tasks include

- ➢ the preparation and filing of United States trademark and copyright applications and renewal applications
- ➢ the preparation and filing of foreign trademark applications and renewal applications
- ➢ the filing of foreign patent applications and the payment of patent annuities required to maintain the patent
- ➢ the execution and legalization of documents required to file a foreign patent or trademark application.

Much of the preliminary research regarding the filing and maintenance for foreign patents and trademark registrations may be conducted by a paralegal to assist the attorney.

Another important role for a paralegal with respect to foreign patent and trademark matters is to ensure that all of the information is communicated effectively between the foreign agent who is handling the patent or trademark application and the attorney. For example, when a letter is received from the foreign agent, the paralegal should look for deadlines in the letter and locate any relevant country information for the attorney's review.

The paralegal should also ensure that the attorney's instructions and comments are communicated to the foreign agent in a timely manner. Follow-up with the foreign agent is crucial to confirm that the foreign agent has received the information required to meet a deadline and to act on that information. Often, a facsimile machine may be out of order or a letter may not arrive.

Another important task of a paralegal is to look ahead on the docket for deadlines to ensure that necessary information and documents are sent in time to the foreign agent.

It is impossible to list all of the tasks that an experienced intellectual property paralegal can perform. Paralegals play an integral role in the successful operation of any intellectual property department.

Chapter One

PATENT BASICS

PATENT LAW IN GENERAL

A patent is a grant of a property right by the government to the inventor that excludes others from making, using, or selling the invention. Patents are granted for a term of 20[1] years (14 years for design patents), which may be extended only by a special act of Congress (except for certain pharmaceutical patents). After expiration of the term, the patentee loses rights to the invention, and it passes into the public domain.

The first patent law was enacted by the United States Congress in 1790.[2] This was soon revised and replaced by the Act of 1793. Since then, Congress has revised or replaced the Patent Statutes in 1836, 1870 and 1952. The Act passed in 1952, United States Code Title 35, remains largely in force today.

One of the most significant developments in United States patent law actually occurred in the federal court system. At one time, patents and related litigation and enforcement questions were handled differently by the separate federal district courts. The same patent that may have been held valid and enforceable by the District Court in Illinois in the Seventh Circuit may have been invalidated by the District Court in Louisiana for the Fifth Circuit. Each jurisdiction had its own standards.

In 1982, the Federal Courts Improvement Act[3] created the Court of Appeals for the Federal Circuit. This court is separate from the other

---

[1] 35 U.S.C. §154 (1952). The GATT legislation (see Chapter Three) was implemented on December 8, 1994, changing the calculation of the term of the patent. If the patent was in force or filed before June 8, 1995, the term of the patent will be 20 years from the filing date. If not, the term will be 17 years from the date of issuance.

[2] Act of April 10, 1790, Chapter 7, 1 Stat. 109

[3] P.L. 97-164, Stat. 25 (April 2 ,1982)

12 federal courts of appeal and has exclusive appellate jurisdiction over cases that arise in whole or in part under the patent laws of the United States.

Title 35 of the United States Code established four conditions for an invention to receive a patent. First, the invention must be in a patentable subject category. Second, the invention must be useful. Third, the invention must be new and original (novel) in comparison to other similar ideas and inventions. Finally, at the time of its creation, the invention must not simply be an obvious improvement to an existing idea that would occur to anyone skilled in the particular area of the idea ("skilled in the art"). The actual prosecution of the patent may take much longer than the idea remains nonobvious.

For example, in 1970 Gilbert Hyatt filed a patent application for a microcontroller. The microcontroller, or microchip, is a computer chip that contains its own software, unlike a microprocessor, which is controlled by external software. Intel is currently one of the more famous manufacturers of the microchip.

Hyatt's patent, No. 4,942,516, did not issue until 1990 after a long and hard-fought battle with the examiners in the United States Patent Office. Unfortunately for Mr. Hyatt, in June 1996 the Patent Office reversed itself, naming Gary Boone and Texas Instruments as the first inventor of the single-chip microcontroller. As of this writing Mr. Hyatt is appealing the reversal.

In general, the inventor must define his or her invention in specific verbal expressions known as **claims** that are filed with the completed application. It is these claims that define the scope of the patent and its enforceability. A patent infringement action will often hinge on the interpretation of a claim in a patent. If the inventor claimed that the process includes the injection of a "coherent stream" of gas, then a stream of gas that is found to be "diffuse" may be held not to infringe the issued patent.

TYPES OF PATENTS

The current United States patent statutes provide for the protection of utility,[4] plant,[5] and design[6] patents (defined later in this chapter). However, neither mathematical formulas nor algorithms for making mathematical computations may be patented. Nor may processes involving "mental" steps be patented if these steps involve subjective reasoning or human judgment. This has led to the controversy as to whether or not computer programs are patentable. It is now held that systems using mathematical formulas can be patented as entire processes. It is common today to find patents composed of claims for computer software structure and methods.

With the passage of the latest revisions to the Patent Act in 1994, the United States implemented a domestic priority system that allows the filing of a provisional application procedure. The provisional application was set up to give the inventor priority rights without triggering the 20-year patent term clock.

After filing a provisional application, the inventor has up to 12 months to file a regular U.S. patent application. The later-filed U.S. patent application uses the provisional application's filing date as a priority date. The 20-year patent term begins with the filing of the regular U.S. application, not with the filing of the provisional application. The priority date is valid not only in the United States, but through the Paris Convention[7], inventors may use the priority date of a U.S. provisional application in other countries.

Provisional applications differ from regular U.S. patent applications. Provisional applications are not published. They are kept in confidence by the Patent and Trademark Office. Since provisional applications are intended to be just an available intermediate step toward a regular U.S. patent application, provisional applications are never examined by the Patent and Trademark Office.

---

[4] 35 U.S.C. § 101
[5] 35 U.S.C. § 161
[6] 35 U.S.C. § 171
[7] Discussed more fully in Chapter Three

For this same reason, provisional applications are automatically abandoned, by operation of law, 12 months after their filing date. If within the 12-month span, a corresponding regular patent application is filed, then such application may claim the provisional application's filing date as the date of priority.

Utility Patents

Title 35 U.S.C. Section 101 states that

> Whoever invents or discovers any new and useful process, machine, manufacture, or composition of matter, or any new and useful improvement thereof, may obtain a patent therefor, subject to the conditions and requirements of this title.

The statute also states that a process "includes a new use of a known process, machine, manufacture, composition of matter, or material."[8]

Utility patents fall into one of four categories:

1. process
2. machine
3. manufacture
4. composition of matter.

These categories were defined in the Act of 1793. The act of 1952 substituted the term "process" for the former term of "art."
In a very general sense, a **process** is a method or proceeding that defines how to do something. The remaining categories are known as "product" categories; that is, they describe a physical embodiment of an invention.

To illustrate, consider Spandex®. The material is "composition of matter," as it contains new and special fibers. The loom on which it is produced is a "machine," and the method for making the material is a "process."

---

[8] 35. U.S.C. § 101(b)

A "manufacture" is a general category used for inventions that do not fall into other categories. Very often, a utility patent will comprise several of these categories.

Utility patents can also claim nonhuman living organisms. In the case of *Diamond v. Chakrabarty*,[9] the Supreme Court allowed the patenting of a process to degrade oil that involved the use of live bacteria. In 1988, the Patent Office issued its first patent for a multicellular animal, a genetically altered mouse[10] described as "a transgenic, non-human mammal."

Plant Patents

In a 1930 revision of the patent law, Congress stated that a patent may be granted to

> Whoever invents or discovers and asexually reproduces any distinct and new variety of plant, including cultivated spores, mutants, hybrids, and newly found seedlings, other than a tuber propagated plant or a plant found in an uncultivated state[11]

Patents are granted to plants that first qualify as plants (multi-celled organisms) as opposed to bacteria and similar single-celled organisms that do not qualify under this section of the Act. The plants must be able to be reproduced asexually, that is, without the benefit of using seeds such as from cuttings or graftings. The plant must also be a new and distinct variety.

In addition, the Patent Office enacted new legislation to comply with the GATT Treaty (refer to full discussion in Chapter Three). This new legislation allowed patent claims for new advances in biotechnology, including patent applications for proteins, DNA molecules, cells, mice, antibodies, and methods of medical treatment among other new advances.

---

[9] 447 U.S. 202 (1980)

[10] U.S. Patent No. 4,736,866 issued on April 12, 1988

[11] 35 U.S.C. § 161

Design Patents

A **design patent** is granted for ornamental elements that are considered to be industrial. The statute states that

> "Whoever invents any new, original, and ornamental
> design for an article of manufacture may obtain a
> patent."[12]

The design, therefore, must be in the nature of an "article of manufacture" that is ornamental and nonfunctional, that is, the design must not perform a function in another process or invention. The design must be purely for aesthetic purposes. If it performs any function at all, it should be the subject of a utility patent.

STATUTORY REQUIREMENTS FOR PATENTS

First to Invent

The United States patent system is unique in the world in that it determines the right to a patent based on determining which inventor was the "first to invent." Section 102(g) of Title 35 of the 1952 Patent Act clarified the rules for determining which inventor was first.

To be granted priority over another inventor, the first inventor must clearly show evidence of the following:

> ➤ the conception of the idea
> ➤ diligence in developing the idea
> ➤ the reduction to practice of the idea.

The invention must be shown to work (reduced to practice) in actual practice or shown to be able to work to receive a patent. If the invention cannot be reduced to practice, then proof of the *conception* determines priority.

---

[12] 35 U.S.C. § 171

In the early days of the Patent Office, an inventor was required to submit a working model of the invention. These inventions were housed on the top floor of the original Patent Office, which is now the National Portrait Gallery in Washington, DC. It is no longer a requirement to submit a working model; however, the inventor must prove that the invention will work as described in the patent application.

Novelty

An invention is considered to be **novel**[13] when it is shown not to be identical to anything disclosed in any prior patent or publication. Novelty is most often measured by comparing the invention, as claimed by the inventor, with the prior art.[14] If the invention is identical to anything found in the prior art, then the invention lacks novelty and is not patentable.

Nonobviousness

To receive a patent, an invention must be original and not obvious to others who work or are otherwise competent in a particular field of knowledge. Generally speaking, an invention is **nonobvious** if comparable prior art does not suggest or instruct the claimed invention and does not provide motivation for a person having ordinary skill in the field to modify the prior art to arrive at the claimed invention.

Nonobviousness[15] is the most important factor in determining whether or not an invention is patentable. The patent examiner will use both the claims submitted in the patent application and the content of the prior art submitted by the inventor, along with any known art, to determine whether the invention is obvious.

---

[13] 35 U.S.C. § 102(a)

[14] The term "prior art" refers to the body of knowledge in the same field as the invention that was available to the public prior to the date of invention.

[15] 35 U.S.C. § 103

STATUTORY BARS FROM RECEIVING A PATENT

Section 102 of the Patent Act describes the bars to receiving a patent in the United States. An invention will be considered to be patentable if it avoids any of the obstructions detailed in this section of the Act.

Known or Used by Others[16]

An inventor may not receive a patent for any invention that was, prior to the applicant's invention date, known or used by another in the United States. If someone has already demonstrated use of the invention in a public manner, then no one can claim the invention after that public use. For example, a person cannot receive a patent for a new type of garden hose nozzle if the same type of nozzle was featured at a home and garden show the year before.

However, the prior use must be **"known,"** that is, it must be public. Secret and private uses of an invention are not enough to stop someone from receiving a patent. An invention may be known, even if it has not been reduced to practice by the inventor. An idea described in an unpublished paper that is available to the public is considered to be "known."

On Sale[17]

A patent application must be placed on file within one year of being placed on sale in the United States. Any actual sale or offer to sell an embodiment of an invention will start the on-sale clock running for the next 365 days. An actual sale is not required. Any offering or bid involving the invention may be sufficient to create the "on sale" date.

---

[16] 35 U.S.C. § 102(a)
[17] 35 U.S.C. § 102(b)

Public Use[18]

Financial transactions involving the invention are not the only way to create a bar to obtaining a patent. Any public, non-experimental use of the invention can create a bar. The courts have recognized an exception for experimental uses of the invention.[19] The public use and on-sale dates do not apply if the use of the invention was primarily for experimentation to test the invention. Public use of the invention outside the United States does apply to United States patent applications.

Abandonment[20]

Use outside the United States may, however, result in abandonment of the invention within the United States. An inventor abandons the invention when he or she relinquishes all rights to obtain a patent in an invention. Delay in applying for a patent does not necessarily imply abandonment, but a patent examiner may infer abandonment from an extended period of unexplained delay.

Not the Inventor (Derivation)[21]

An applicant will not receive a patent on an invention if it is determined that the applicant derived the invention from some other person or information source. This bar concerns the originality of the idea that is the subject of the invention. If the invention is not wholly the original idea of the applicant, then the applicant is not entitled to a patent on the entire idea submitted in the application. A person will not be granted a patent on an invention he or she did not create.

---

[18] 35 U.S.C. § 102(b)

[19] *City of Elizabeth v. American Nicholson Pavement Company*, 97 U.S. 126 (1878)

[20] 35 U.S.C. § 102(c)

[21] 35 U.S.C. § 102(f)

Prior Invention[22]

A patent will not be granted to an inventor if it is proved that the invention is already the subject of an earlier invention by another person. The first inventor must not have abandoned, suppressed or concealed the invention from the public. This section is the source of some controversy, as it is very similar to the consideration of prior art as a bar and is very difficult to distinguish from the definition of prior art.

CHAPTER QUESTIONS

Patent Basics

1.   Explain the nature of a patented invention as it differs from other types of intellectual property.

2.   Outline and define the three types of patents granted in the United States.

3.   An inventor has approached you with a new concept for a machine part. Explain the requirements for obtaining a U.S. patent under current law, along with the bars that prevent a person from receiving a patent.

---

[22] 35 U.S.C. § 102(g)

Chapter Two

THE U.S. PATENT APPLICATION

ELEMENTS OF THE U.S. PATENT APPLICATION

The drafting of a patent application is a complex task. Although applicants may file applications themselves and represent themselves before the Patent Office, it is often best to secure the assistance of a licensed patent attorney. Patent attorneys are usually degreed engineers who have become lawyers. They also must pass a special test to be licensed to practice before the Patent Office. This test is known as the Patent Bar examination.

The drafter of a patent application must understand the technology involved in an invention and characterize this invention clearly and completely for the patent examiner. The elements of the application must fully disclose the invention. Nothing important must be left out or left to the imagination of the reader of the issued patent.

These elements must provide sufficient information about the invention to allow any other person "skilled in the art" to "make and use the same invention."[1] It must clearly show others in the same field how to duplicate the invention exactly; and it must also disclose the best mode known to the inventor for practicing the invention (see page 14). This is important, because at the end of the patent's term, the invention passes into the public domain. Unlike completed trademark applications, which are public record to protect the applicant's rights to the invention, the Patent Office holds applications in confidence until the patent is issued.

United States patent applications consist of several parts, the most fundamental of which appear in the final **issued patent**. The essential

---

[1] 35 U.S.C. § 112

elements of the patent applications are best understood by an examination of the individual sections of the final issued patent.

The issued patent is divided into five sections:

1. the front page and abstract
2. the drawings
3. the background and summary of the invention
4. the preferred embodiment
5. the claims.

Front Page and Abstract of the Issued Patent

The front page of the patent displays in a concise manner many of the important aspects of the patent. The front page contains

- the patent number
- the title
- a list of the inventors
- the application information
- the International and U.S. Classifications
- the range of the search conducted by the examiner
- the list of prior art cited
- the number of claims and figures in the patent
- the abstract.

The abstract is a concise paragraph that briefly describes the workings and features of the invention. It allows the reader to summarize the major points of the invention in connection with the other information found on the front page of the patent. Using this information as search criteria is an extremely effective tool in patent searching.

Information Disclosure Statement

The applicant and all the persons associated with the application have a "duty of candor"[2] in connection with the application. That means the inventor must disclose information to the Patent Office that is directly

---

[2] 37 C.F.R. § 1.56

relevant to the invention and must not misrepresent any facts relevant to the invention or any known prior art.

An applicant may submit an Information Disclosure Statement that lists any patents and publications that he or she feels are relevant to the invention and its patentability. This statement is not a requirement but is strongly encouraged by the Patent Office as a way to comply with the duty of candor. The statement must explain any listed item's relevance to the invention. It may be updated as new information is found during the prosecution of the application.

The Drawings

The drawings used to depict the invention are found immediately following the front page. Each page may have one or many figures representing various views of the invention or, possibly, alternate designs. The figures are referenced mainly from the "Preferred Embodiment" section of the patent.

Drawings are not always required.[3] They are submitted when an illustration is necessary to fully explain the workings and scope of the invention. For example, drawings are usually required for mechanical and electrical inventions. Chemical patents do not typically require a drawing, as the composition of the chemical being patented can be fully described by accepted language and formulas.

The Background and Summary

This background section is included in the patent as an overview of the existing technology in the same field as the invention. It discusses the advantages and disadvantages of this prior art in relation to the invention. The summary lists the ways in which the invention is a novel improvement over the existing technology. It points out the invention's superiority and differences from what had existed before.

---

[3] 37 C.F.R. § 1.81(a)

The Preferred Embodiment (Best Mode)

This section contains a detailed listing of the invention. The invention is described in detail. Every part of the invention is referred to and numbered in one of the accompanying drawings. The section must set forth the "best mode contemplated by the inventor for carrying out the invention."[4] The inventor must disclose the ideal conditions (that is "best mode") for operating the invention. This requirement prevents inventors from obtaining patents on inventions while keeping the best method of its operation a secret from the public.

The Claims

The most important part in determining the scope of the patent is its claims. A claim is one grammatically correct sentence. This is where the invention is actually defined. Patent litigation and enforcement often hinge on what is set out in the claims. The claims must describe the elements of the invention in a sequential manner from some frame of reference. The claims focus on the interrelationship of elements.

There are two types of claims, independent and dependent. An **independent claim** stands on its own and does not refer to another claim. By contrast, a **dependent claim** refers to an independent claim or other dependent claim. These claims form a chain of dependency and, taken together as a unit, fully describe the invention.

Below is an example of an independent claim from U.S. Patent No. 3,573,454 granted to Andersen, *et al.*, entitled "Method and Apparatus for Ion Bombardment Using Negative Ions."

> 1. Method of implanting particles of atomic dimension in a specimen of an electrically insulating material comprising the step of bombarding the specimen with negatively charged ions, imparting energy to the ions at a value selected to cause them to drive secondary electrons out of the specimen to remove negative charges at a rate to compensate fully for the negative

---

[4] 35 U.S.C. § 112

charges carried to the surface of the specimen by the ions thereby to avoid the accumulation of an excessive negative electrical charge on the surface of the specimen.

A dependent claim for this patent would begin "The method in Claim 1 in which ...."

Fees

The fees of the U.S. Patent Office are fairly substantial. As of October 1, 1997, the basic filing fee for an application was $790. However, individual inventors, small businesses, universities and nonprofit organizations are classified as "small entities"[5] and qualify for a 50 percent discount on the fees.

THE LIFE OF A U.S. PATENT APPLICATION

A patent examiner may reject any or all of the claims submitted in a patent application. The inventor may then, through an attorney, reply by offering either to amend the claims or submit evidence to support all the allegations of the claims. The examiner will review the written response and evaluate the new information. Hearings and interviews may be held between the examiner and the applicant. This exchange between the examiner and the inventor is part of the "prosecution" of the application.

Initial Application

A patent application has four parts, namely:

1. the specification of the invention, including at least one claim
2. a drawing
3. the inventor's oath or declaration[6] attesting to the contents of the patent application

---

[5] 37 C.F.R. § 1.9 (c), (d), and (e)

[6] Declaration may be used instead of oaths; a declaration does not require the signature of a notary.

4.   the filing fees.

The specification and drawings must be submitted in order to receive a filing date.[7] The oath and the filing fees may be submitted at a later date.[8]

After filing, patent applications in the Patent and Trademark Office are classified by technology area and assigned for examination. The U.S. Patent Office uses a classification system of over 400 classes and subclasses to categorize the different areas of inventions. A summary of the main U.S. classes is attached at Appendix Table 7.

The classification system allows the examiner to define the subject matter of the patent application precisely. For example, an inventor may have developed a new hospital bed that can be used for x-ray purposes. Class 5 is the category for beds in general. However, you can have a folding bed, or a truck bed, or a flower planting bed. The examiner must rely on the subclasses of Class 5 to clarify the scope of the invention. An example of some of the subclasses for Class 5 are:

001.00 MISCELLANEOUS	600.00 INVALID BED OR
002.10 COMBINATION	SURGICAL SUPPORT
FURNITURE	601.00 . . Adapted for x-raying
002.00 . . . Table beds	602.00 . . Adapted for birthing
002.00 . . . Outfolding sides	602.00 . . Adapted for infant support
005.00 . . . Unfolding top	602.00 . . Having toilet means
006.00 . . . Folding bed enclosed	605.00 . . Having flushing means
007.00 . . . Sofa form	606.00 . . Having drain means

From this short list, it is apparent that the new hospital bed would fall into subclasses 2.10, 6, 600 and 601, among others in the subclasses. The classification of a patent defines the scope of the area of prior art that will be considered in connection with the inventor's application.

----

[7] 35 U.S.C. § 102(b)
[8] 37 C.F.R. § 1.53(d)

Responses to Office Actions[9]

A patent examiner normally reviews the application in the order in which it was received. This shows the importance of obtaining a filing date. The examination consists of a study of the application for compliance with the legal requirements and a search through United States patents, prior foreign patent documents, and available literature.

A decision is reached by the examiner based on the results of this search. The first formal correspondence from the Patent Office concerning the patentability of the invention is in the form of a first "office action." This action is generally received about nine months after the application is filed.

The first office action will usually contain reasons why the examiner does not believe that the application should be granted as a patent. If the invention as claimed is not considered patentable subject matter, the claims will be rejected.

It is not uncommon for some or all of the claims to be rejected in the first action by the examiner. Patent attorneys usually try to file the claims broadly to increase the scope of the patent's protection. The examiner will usually try to limit the scope of the claims to the actual invention.

In responding to the first office action, the applicant should specifically address the perceived errors or omissions in the examiner's office action. Frequently, the amendment will include an amendment to the claims in order to clarify the invention and to overcome the prior art cited in the first office action. In addition to the amendment, the document may contain arguments as to how the amended claims are patentable.

The response of an applicant to an action by the office must be made before a prescribed deadline. Typically, the deadline is set three months after the office action is mailed and can be extended one month

---

[9] The applicant may petition to have the application made special and, if this petition is granted, the application will be examined on a priority basis.

at a time up to six months. Each one-month extension requires the payment of an additional fee. If no reply to the office action is received before the six-month deadline, the application is considered abandoned.

Understanding Claims (Charting Claims)

As mentioned above, there are two types of claims in a patent application: independent and dependent. A patent attorney will divide the invention into essential and nonessential elements.

> ➤   The **essential elements** are the parts of the invention that are required for the minimum functioning of the device. These become the independent claims.

> ➤   The **nonessential elements** are the parts that assist the functioning of the device, but are not required for minimum functioning of the device. These elements form the dependent claims. Dependent claims are easily identified, as they reference another earlier claim.

Claims are either allowed, objected to, or rejected by the patent examiner. In response, the applicant may either argue the worth of the claim as filed, modify the claim, or cancel the claim by either dropping it from the application or rewriting it and reintroducing it as a new claim. It is important to remember that a claim is only numbered once, and the others do not shift their numbers if an earlier claim is cancelled or dropped. Claim 1 will always be claim 1, and claim 2 will always be claim 2, even if claim 1 is dropped.

One of the most efficient ways of keeping track of the life of the claims is to produce a flowchart of the claims. Take as an example a patent application with five claims shown in the following figure.

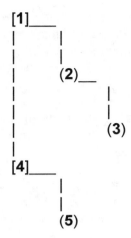

Claims 1 and 4 are independent. These are represented in a straight line
under each other in square boxes. Claim 2 is dependent on Claim 1 and
is shown in a circle under Claim 1. Claim 3 is dependent on Claim 2
and is shown in a chain under Claim 2. Finally, Claim 5 is dependent
on Claim 4 and shown connected under it. Independent claims are
shown in offset chains, while dependent claims are shown in chains
under the independent.

This method graphically illustrates the claims and their relationship to
each other and is modified to show the progress during prosecution. All
the claims are renumbered in sequence by the Patent Office when the
final version of the patent application is approved for registration.

Continuation and Continuation-In-Part Applications

After a response is filed by the applicant, the application will be
reconsidered by the examiner. The applicant will be notified if claims
or any other part of the application are rejected. This second office
action is usually made "in final." In making such final rejection, the
examiner repeats or states all grounds of rejection considered
applicable to the claims in the application. If an application is rejected
in final, the applicant may appeal the decision to the Board of Patent
Appeals and Interferences.

As an alternative to an appeal, an applicant can request consideration of different claims or further evidence by filing a new continuation application. The new application requires a filing fee. The applicant may file for new consideration of the entire application. This is known as a **continuation application**. It is also possible to file for consideration of only a section of the original application (see Divisional Applications below). If the applicant adds new matter to the section of the original application, the application is known as a **continuation-in-part** application.

If the continuation or continuation-in-part application is filed before expiration of the six-month response period for the final office action, the applicant will be entitled to the earlier filing date for subject matter common to both applications.

Divisional Applications

If two or more inventions are claimed in a single application, and are regarded by the Patent Office to be of such a nature that a single patent should not be issued for both of them, then the applicant will be required to limit the application to one of the inventions. The other invention may be made the subject of a separate application that, if filed while the first application is still pending, will be entitled to the benefit of the filing date of the first application. This separate application is referred to as a **divisional application.**

Interferences by Third Parties

During the prosecution of an application, another inventor may raise a question as to who originated an idea first. If a party feels that it has prior rights to an invention, it may file an **interference proceeding** with the Board of Patent Interferences.[10] Interferences are complex proceedings that suspend the prosecution of a patent application until the question of priority is decided.

---

[10] 37 C.F.R. §§ 1.601 - 1.688

Petitions to Revive

If the patent application becomes abandoned for any reason, an applicant may file a Petition to Revive the application with the appropriate fee. If the reason for abandonment was the late filing of a document, then usually a fee may be paid and the application reinstated.

Publication and Issuance of Final Registration

When the Patent and Trademark Office allows a patent to be issued, another fee, the **issuance fee,** is required. This fee changes on a regular basis. The patent is then issued, and a notification of the issuance is published in the Official Gazette of the Patent and Trademark Office. Unlike trademark publication, the publication of a patent is the first and final notice to the public of the existence of the patent application. Prior to the issuance, the application is held in confidence.

POSTISSUANCE MATTERS

Reexamination

A person (including the inventor) who believes that a patent was granted in error may file a request that the patent be reexamined for validity.[11] Any reexamination is conducted under the same rules and procedures as the original examination of the patent application. However, only the **patentee** (owner of the patent being reexamined) may participate in the reexamination process. These proceedings are usually initiated at the request of a third party who is being sued by the patentee for infringement of the issued patent. The intended outcome of the reexamination process is usually to cancel the granted patent, although a patentee may also try to strengthen patent claims through this procedure.

---

[11] 35 U.S.C. § 304

Reissuance

On occasion, a patentee may feel that a patent was granted containing errors. In this instance, a patentee may request that a patent be corrected through additional examination to clarify and sharpen any omissions or errors that appear in the final issued patents.[12]

If the request to reissue the patent is filed within two years of the grant date, the scope of the claims may be broadened beyond the original patent. However, if the request to reissue is filed after the first two years, then the scope of the claims may not be broadened. The intended outcome of this proceeding is to have the patent reissued with the corrections.

Maintenance Fees

After a patent is issued, the protection provided is technically for 20 years from the date of application. In order to receive the full 20[13] years of patent protection, the owner of the patent must pay three periodic maintenance fees at three, seven, and eleven years. Each of these periodic maintenance fees is larger than the previous fee.

When the patent expires, it passes into the public domain. The increase in the maintenance fee is to encourage the patent owner to make sure the patent is still of value to him or her. If not, the patent owner may let the patent lapse early, and it will pass into public use.

If the maintenance fee is not paid on time, the Patent and Trademark Office provides a six-month grace period in which to make the payment. Thus the maintenance fee may actually be paid at 3½, 7½, and 11½ years.

---

[12] 35 U.S.C. § 305

[13] The GATT (refer to Chapter Three) legislation was implemented on December 8, 1994, changing the calculation of the term of the patent. If the patent was in force or filed before June 8, 1995, the term of the patent will be 20 years from the filing date. Further, if there is a parent application (see continuation applications above), the term will be calculated from the filing date of the earliest (or first) application in the patent continuation family. This does not affect design patents, which remain at a term of 14 years.

CHAPTER QUESTIONS

The U.S. Patent Application

1.   Describe the elements of a United States patent application. Which of these elements are usually included but are not required by current law?

2.   Explain the course of a patent application in the United States Patent Office.

3.   Why would a party file a divisional application? How does this differ from a continuation and continuation-in-part application?

4.   What is a patent claim? Explain the difference between an independent and dependent claim.

Chapter Three

THE INTERNATIONAL
PATENT

INTERNATIONAL PATENT CONCEPTS

Patent protection granted to an inventor by a government is only valid in the country where the inventor requested it. The rights do not extend beyond that country. A U.S. patent will only grant rights to the inventor within the 50 states and the United States territories.

An inventor may apply for patents in other countries. Similarly, foreign inventors may apply for patents within the United States. However, the United States has enacted the Invention Secrecy Act.[1] The Act states that any invention made in the United States is subject to licensing permission from the Commissioner of Patents and Trademarks.

Attempting to pursue patent protection individually in several countries is complex and expensive, since each country has its unique patent laws and practices. Important elements in patent laws and practices vary significantly from country to country, and differences among various nations are being negotiated. In any foreign patent filing it is best to consult with a patent agent in each country to ensure that all requirements are met.

For the interests of U.S. national security, a U.S. inventor must either obtain a license to file foreign applications from the U.S. Patent Commissioner or must wait six months after filing a U.S. application. The six-month interval allows the PTO to examine the application to determine whether it involves any national security interests.

If there are national security interests involved, then the PTO will issue a secrecy order and prevent any foreign applications for the invention.

---

[1] 35 U.S.C. §§ 181-188

Filing an application with the PTO is considered to be an application
for a license to file in other countries.

Priority

The first filing of an application for any invention may be in any
country. A patent application in the United States may be filed within
12 months of the filing of another application for the same invention in
another country.[2] If certain conditions are met, the U.S. filing may
claim the priority (or benefit of) the earlier filing date.

Essentially, the earlier application must have been filed in a country
that grants "similar privileges" to an application filed in the United
States. The countries include, but are not limited to, the Paris
Convention member countries. A priority application is entitled to the
"same effect" as an application filed in the United States. This is
important for the concept of prior art in the examination of a priority
U.S. application.

For example, if an inventor files a utility application in the United
States on January 1, 1997, that same inventor may file applications in a
country belonging to the Paris Convention for up to 12 months,[3] that is
January 1, 1999, and receive the privileges of "priority." The later
filings will be considered to have the original January 1, 1997, filing
date. This could prove quite useful if a competitor filed in another
country before January 1, 1998.

The priority date of the foreign application is the date when the
invention is made to be workable in real-world applications. This date
becomes the effective date for cutting off prior art references. If
anything is discovered that might endanger the patent application and it
is dated after the invention priority date, then it is not considered by the
examiner.

---

[2] 35 U.S.C. § 119
[3] Six months for design patents

INTERNATIONAL PATENT CLASSIFICATION (IPC) SYSTEM

The International Patent Classification (IPC) system is used by most countries in classifying their patent documents and is administered by the World Intellectual Property Organization (WIPO). It is a different classification system than the one used in the United States, although they have similar appearances. The IPC has a hierarchical structure and is primarily based on the principle of function. The classification schedule is divided into eight main sections, each of which is further broken down into classes, subclasses, main groups, and subgroups.

The IPC is currently in its fifth edition (1989). Revisions to the IPC take effect once every five years, but many revision projects are continuously negotiated by various international committees. Nearly all countries use the IPC system except the U.S., which uses its own national classification system. The European Patent Office uses its own European Classification (ECLA) system, which is based on IPC but offers a more detailed breakdown of the subject matter.

PARIS CONVENTION FOR THE PROTECTION OF INDUSTRIAL PROPERTY

The meeting known as the Paris Convention was first held in 1883 to adopt a treaty providing the foundation for international patent protection. The treaty has gone through many revisions over the years. As of January 1993, 108 countries were members of the Paris Convention Agreement. The agreement applies broadly and includes all forms of intellectual property. Its membership is open to all countries.

The treaty signifies two important provisions:

1. Each member country guarantees citizens of other countries the same rights as its own citizens.
2. The treaty grants the right of priority (the "priority date" – see above).

Therefore, if an inventor files an application in a member country of the Paris Convention, other member countries will honor that first filing date. In this way, an inventor who wants protection in multiple countries need not file all applications at the same time. Rather, the inventor has 12 months from the first application to decide on subsequent filings in Paris Convention member countries. Appendix Table 2 lists the current Paris Convention member countries.

PATENT COOPERATION TREATY (PCT)

The Patent Cooperation Treaty, concluded in 1970, has been in effect since 1978. The treaty has gone through several revisions since then and is currently administered by WIPO. Originally only 40 countries were signatories to the treaty; but as of January 1994, 128 countries belong to the PCT. Appendix Table 2 lists the current PCT countries.

The major accomplishment of the treaty has been the establishment of two provisions:

1.   It established centralized filing procedures for international patent applications.

2.   It established the treaty standardized application format. This simplifies the procedure for filing multiple applications for a patent on the same invention and simplifies complex issues surrounding international patent protection.

WIPO[4] publishes the *PCT Applicant's Guide* that provides detailed information for inventors interested in filing a PCT application. The guide includes specific requirements of each of the patent offices, a list of the PCT member countries, receiving offices, international searching authorities, and samples of various application forms. The *Guide* is usually updated in January and July of each year. It is available in English, French, Chinese, German, and Japanese editions.

---

[4] P.O. Box 18, CH-1211
34, Chemin des Colombettes, Geneva 20 Switzerland

EUROPEAN PATENT CONVENTION (EPC)

The European Patent Convention (EPC) provides a single procedure for granting one "European patent" to an invention that, upon payment of an appropriate fee, will be valid in all EPC member countries. Only one application is necessary to obtain protection in all EPC member countries, thus avoiding multiple filing fees. Once granted, the European patent has the same value and is subject to the same conditions as the national patent granted by that country.

The patent application may be filed at the European Patent Office in Munich, or at the department in The Hague, or at a branch agency of the department. If the laws of the contracting countries allow, it can also be filed at the Central Service of Industrial Property in these countries.

To be valid in the designated countries, a granted EPO patent must conform to the laws of each individual country. For example, in some countries it is necessary to file the translation of the text in the official language of that country. If the translation is not filed within a certain time limit, the patent application is considered to be abandoned in that particular country.

Currently, the member countries of the European Patent Convention are:

- Albania
- Austria
- Belgium
- Denmark
- Finland
- France
- Germany
- Great Britain
- Greece
- Ireland
- Italy
- Latvia
- Liechtenstein
- Lithuania
- Luxembourg
- Netherlands
- Portugal
- Monaco
- Romania
- Spain
- Slovenia
- Sweden
- Switzerland

GENERAL AGREEMENT ON TARIFFS
AND TRADE (GATT)

The recently enacted agreement on the Uruguay round of negotiations
to revise the General Agreement on Tariffs and Trade (GATT)
provides a new framework within which to operate, namely, the World
Trade Organization (WTO), which has its headquarters in Geneva,
Switzerland.

GATT has affected international patent and intellectual property law.
The general provisions of GATT's Agreement on Trade Related
Intellectual Property Issues (TRIPS) follow those of the Paris and Bern
Conventions, providing for national treatment and most-favored-nation
treatment. This is subject, however, to the exceptions to these
principles that already exist in these conventions. That is to say,
member states must not discriminate in favor of their own citizens
against the patent, trademark, and copyright rights of foreigners who
are citizens of other GATT member countries, nor favor the rights of
citizens of one member country over the rights of citizens of another.

CHAPTER QUESTIONS

The International Patent

1.   What is an international patent, and how may one apply to
receive protection around the world?

2.   What is the IPC, and what body current administers its
maintenance?

3.   Compare and contrast the Patent Cooperation Treaty and the
European Patent Convention.

EXERCISES

A.   Compose memos recommending a course of action for you and
        your attorney concerning the following fact patterns. Be certain
        to address questions about forms and procedures needed, as

well as the research tools (refer to Appendix Tables 1 and 2) needed to accomplish each project.

1. A person claims to have invented a new way of calculating fractions. She also tells you that she has worked for years on this matter alone and can prove all her work.

2. A fashion designer shows you a new style of earrings. The pair is distinctive and very unusual. The earrings are a standard clip design in the way they attach to the ears. The designer wants to file in Europe, particularly France, for the Paris fashion markets.

3. Two inventors have approached your firm claiming that they have developed a new method for manufacturing spark plugs for automobiles. They want their invention to be owned by a small company they have just formed. They have also received inquiries from manufacturers in Japan, England, Australia, Germany and Thailand, and would like to begin the patenting process in those countries.

B. Referring to a copy of U.S. Patent No. 3,573,454 granted to Andersen, *et al.*, entitled "Method and Apparatus for Ion Bombardment Using Negative Ions" complete the following exercises:

1. List the elements of the front page of the '454 patent.
2. List the inventors and assignee of the patent.
3. Indicate whether or not the patent is in force.
4. Chart the claims of the '454 patent.

Chapter Four

TRADEMARK BASICS

TRADEMARK LAW IN GENERAL

Trademarks, patents and copyrights are similar in that they are all referred to as "intellectual property," property that is not tangible but that has value to its owner. All three types of intellectual property differ from one another. Unlike copyrights or patents, trademark rights can last for as long as the owner continues to use the mark to identify its goods or services. Currently, the term of a federal trademark registration is 10 years, with 10-year renewal terms.

The public learns, through purchasing experience, that goods or services bearing a mark come from a single source and will meet an expectation of a standard of quality that the goods or services sold under the mark have met in the past. This predictability of a level of quality and reassurance of a known source provides the owner or user of the mark with the benefit of goodwill held by the public for the product or service that the owner offers. This goodwill is often the basis of the owner's business.

People return to a McDonald's restaurant, for example, expecting a certain level of service and quality of meal. If their budgets will allow, consumers will most likely choose a Cadillac over a Yugo. However, McDonald's and Cadillac would not have their business integrity if it were not for their reputation among consumers.

Trademarks identify the source of the goods or services being offered. A label on a pair of jeans or the name on the "For Sale" sign in front of a house can either bring in customers or send them away, depending on the reputation that name has with the public. The value of a name on a product helps one dishwashing soap sell better than the next on a store shelf.

The source of the goods or services can even be anonymous to the public. For example, purchasers attach different levels of quality and performance to the CLINIQUE® and ESTEE LAUDER® brands of cosmetics. They are often sold in competition with each other. Both brands are, however, made by the same manufacturer.

United States Trademark Law

On July 8, 1870, the Congress of the United States passed the first federal act providing for trademark registration. The act was entitled An Act to Revise, Consolidate and Amend the Statutes Relating to Patents and Copyrights. This act was overturned and replaced by the Act of March 3, 1881. Since then, numerous new trademark acts and amendments have been enacted. The most notable amendments have occurred on February 20, 1905, March 19, 1920, and July 5, 1946.

The revision of July 5, 1946, was called the Lanham Act[1] and remains in effect today. It has been revised and amended over 20 times, including a revision signed into law in 1997. The first trademark in the United States was granted to the Averill Chemical Paint Company on October 15, 1870, for a design placed on containers for liquid paint.

Trademark rights in the United States are generally obtained through use of a mark. Registration is not required in order for trademark rights to exist. A federal registration issued by the U.S. Patent and Trademark Office (Trademark Office) is a recognition of a trademark owner's rights acquired through use of the mark. The owner of a federal registration is presumed to be the owner of the mark for the goods and/or services specified in the registration and is entitled to use the mark nationwide.

A party cannot maintain a federal registration without using the mark in the United States. If use is continued, then a registration may be renewed at each 10-year interval. For example, the oldest valid federal registration is No. 11,210 for SAMSON and design for cords, lines, twines and ropes. This mark was originally registered on May 27, 1884. It was last renewed on October 11, 1994, by Samson Ocean

---

[1] 15 U.S.C. § 1051

Systems, Inc., and will be valid until May 27, 2004. The registration claims a first use date in U.S. commerce of January 1, 1884.

Trademarks are also registerable at the state level in all fifty states. However, federal registration provides a broader scope of protection for a trademark than a state registration.

TYPES OF TRADEMARKS

Traditionally, a trademark is a word, phrase, symbol, design, or combination of these elements that identifies and distinguishes the goods and services of one party from those of any other party. A **service mark** is the same as a trademark except that it identifies and distinguishes services rather than products. Normally, a trademark appears on the product or on its packaging, while a service mark appears in advertising and promotional literature for the service.

There are, however, many non-alphanumeric trademarks and service marks. For example, NBC has registered the three tones it first used in connection with its radio broadcasts. Corning has registered a certain shade of pink to identify its home insulation products.

Protection may also be granted to marks that identify membership in an organization or certification by an association for quality, such as the "Good Housekeeping" seal. These are known as **certification marks.**

Marks are used to indicate the origin of the supplier of goods or services. Similar or even identical marks may be used for different goods and services as long as the public would not be confused that there was a single source for the product or services. For example, the mark COMET® is registered both by The Proctor and Gamble Company for a household cleanser and by Jack Godfrey & Sons, Inc., for dry cleaning and laundry services.

Trademarks[2]

A trademark identifies a tangible good or product of a company or individual. Trademarks are marks that can be placed directly on the product or its packaging. To determine if a name is a trademark (rather than a "service mark," discussed later) try to imagine whether or not you could put a sticker with the mark on the product. If you can, then the mark is likely a trademark.

Trade Names

As late as the first two decades of the 20th century, the term "trade name" was used to describe any mark that was highly descriptive of the goods or services (AT A GLANCE® calendars), geographically descriptive (RHODE ISLAND RED® hot dogs), or contained a personal name (FAMOUS AMOS® cookies). However, since a 1926[3] Supreme Court decision, the term **trade name** refers to an actual name of a business rather than the goods or services that business may provide. For example, Exxon Corporation is a trade name, and EXXON® is a trademark used to identify the company's products and services.

Service Marks[4]

As the name implies, a service mark identifies the services of a provider. Marks used by a company or individual can function as both trademarks and service marks. GUESS® can refer both to the clothing in International Class 25 and to the retail store services in International Class 42. The public comes to learn to expect a certain quality standard from every franchise location of a fast food restaurant chain, for example, that bears the same name or service mark.

---

[2] 15 U.S.C. § 1052

[3] *American Steel Foundries v. Robertson*, 46 S.Ct. 160 (1926)

[4] 15 U.S.C. § 1053

Designs Used as Trademarks

As far back as the Greek civilization, craftsmen used designs to identify
their products and businesses. In a largely illiterate society, designs
were an easy way to recognize the work of, say, one potter from
another. This same concept was used in the guilds of the Middle Ages.
When someone saw a sign with a sheep hanging from a ribbon, they
knew that the person was a member of the guild of wool merchants.

Designs work in much the same way today. They help the public to
make a nonverbal association of a mark with the goods and services of
others. Many would agree that the "golden arches" carry as much
weight as the "McDonald's" name for the restaurant chain.

It is also possible for the actual configuration of a product to serve as a
trademark. Many people recognize the COCA-COLA® bottle shape. In
1960 the Trademark Office in the United States registered the bottle
shape as being a trademark for the cola product it contained. Many
configurations have been recognized as trademarks, including
restaurant designs.[5]

Certification Marks and Collective Marks[6]

In the United States, marks can also refer to a standard of quality for a
product. The Lanham Act of 1946 introduced two new types of marks
into U.S. trademark practice, certification marks and **collective marks**.

Many companies try to get THE GOOD HOUSEKEEPING SEAL for
their products, just as fisheries want THE CATFISH INSTITUTE to
certify the quality of their grown fish. These marks indicate that the
certified products meet a standard of excellence set by the reviewing
board.

Similarly, a collective mark signifies affiliation with an organization
that has set certain standards for membership. This standard can range

---

[5] *Taco Cabana Inc v. Two Pesos, Inc.,* 932 F.2d 1113 (5th Cir. 1991)
aff'd 112 S.Ct. 2753 (1992).
[6] 15 U.S.C. § 1054

from simply paying dues, to belonging to a group such as a museum or philanthropic organization, to passing a series of tests to show proficiency in a field, such as a *Certified Public Accountant.* Membership in unions may also be covered by collective marks.

Strong Versus Weak Marks

The scope of protection afforded a trademark in the marketplace depends upon the strength and unique quality of the mark. For example, does the mark stand out in the crowd or does it blend in and sound like all the other marks in the business field. The marks that stand out are strong, the ones that blend in are weaker.

Fanciful Marks

Fanciful marks are marks that have been invented or "coined" for a particular product or service. They consist of original terms. One of the best examples of an original term belongs to a petrochemical company. In an effort to develop one of the strongest marks possible, a merged group of oil companies primarily known as Esso Oil Corporation went to great lengths to ensure that their new name EXXON® had no meaning in any language.

Arbitrary Marks

Common names can function as arbitrary marks when they are taken out of context. While using the term "banana" to describe a banana is generic, the term can be used out of context and function as an effective trademark. A good illustration of this concept occurred when Newton's Apple shortened its name for its computer to APPLE. The company formerly known as Overseas Products International Incorporated used the term "Fossil" for its new line of watches. Neither name was new to the language, but they had no recognized meaning in the context of computers or watches.

Fanciful or arbitrary marks are considered the "strongest" of trademarks, as they are the most removed from the product or service they represent. Therefore, it is highly unlikely that another company would adopt such a mark for the exact same product or service.

Fanciful or arbitrary marks are considered "inherently distinctive"[7] trademarks when they are first used and are entitled to a broad scope of protection.

Suggestive Marks

As the term implies, a suggestive mark hints at the nature of the goods or services being offered. The purchasers of L'EGGS® pantyhose, for example, would be able to guess from the name that the product had something to do with a person's leg. A suggestive mark is also considered "inherently distinctive" and does not have to demonstrate any recognition with the public to function as a trademark. This "recognition" with the public is referred to in trademark law parlance as **secondary meaning**.

Merely Descriptive Marks

A mark is termed **merely descriptive** if it characterizes the purpose, nature, or use of the goods or services it represents. For example, the Trademark Office has held that "interactive toys" is merely descriptive of computer games for children.

Merely descriptive marks are not considered "inherently distinctive" and, therefore, are not entitled to protection as a trademark when they are first used. Once the term has been extensively used and promoted, the public recognizes the term as the trademark of one party, and the term is protectable as a trademark. This public recognition of the merely descriptive term as a trademark is referred to as "secondary meaning."

The Trademark Office traditionally accepts five years of continuous use of the "merely descriptive" term as evidence that the term has acquired a secondary meaning and functions as a trademark. In the absence of five years' use of the mark, evidence of a heavy saturation of advertising will generally convince the Trademark Office that the term has acquired a secondary meaning. For example, a $50 million campaign introducing the mark to the public over a six-month period of

---

[7] *Two Pesos v. Taco Cabana, id.*

time would quickly educate the public to recognize the term as the trademark of one party.

Registration of a merely descriptive trademark will be refused by the Trademark Office unless the applicant can demonstrate that the mark has acquired secondary meaning.

Applications to register "Shear Pleasure" for beauty salons, "Quik Print" for printing services and "Rite-Fit" for furniture slip covers are examples of descriptive marks that had to prove secondary meaning. The owners of "Shear Pleasure" were unable to convince the U.S. Trademark Office that the phrase functioned as a trademark. Even Levi Strauss was unsuccessful in convincing the Trademark Office that "Straights" functioned as a trademark for its line of straight-legged jeans.

Marks that are composed of laudatory terms are also considered to be merely descriptive. Terms such as "DELUXE," "SPECIAL," "EXTRA," and "SUPER," are deemed to be concise descriptions of the goods or services represented by the mark and are usually not registerable alone. These types of marks are also known as "puffing" marks.

Generic Terms

A generic term is the commonly recognized name for an entire category of a products or services. Since generic items are usually sold at discount rates, they do not carry any special significance for the product or service and, in fact, imply lesser quality. For example, "purse" is the generic name for a woman's handbag, and "pc" has become the recognized generic name for a personal computer.

Misuse of a trademark by the public can lead to some unexpected consequences, namely **genericide.** Genericide occurs when there is widespread use of a trademark by the public as a generic term so that the trademark no longer identifies the product of only one party. Rather, the public uses the term to identify the product of many different parties in the same line of business.

A trademark can be tremendously valuable to its owner for identification. In a recent study, 92% of consumers recognized the ARM & HAMMER® trademark. This is a level of familiarity that clearly makes this brand stand out when the consumer is choosing which product to take home. On September 1, 1992, *Financial World* magazine published a list of the most valuable trademarks. The top 10, in descending order were, MARLBORO®, COCA-COLA®, BUDWEISER®, PEPSI-COLA®, NESCAFE®, KELLOGG®, WINSTON®, PAMPERS®, CAMEL®, and CAMPBELL®.

Ironically, there is a danger of being too successful with the use of a trademark. It can become a generic word. Marks such as "aspirin,"[8] "escalator,"[9] "trampoline,"[10] "monopoly,"[11] and "dry ice,"[12] have all become generic words for the goods they once represented.

Many companies have taken an aggressive approach to prevent genericide by the public. Kimberly-Clark is actively trying to maintain KLEENEX® as an enforceable trademark for facial tissues, and Sony is trying to maintain WALKMAN® as an enforceable trademark for personal headphone stereos.

For example, the Xerox Corporation has been trying to counteract the public's use of its trademark as a noun or verb. The company has run large campaigns based on the slogan "You can't xerox a Xerox on a xerox." The first and second appearances of the mark show the public's misuse substituting the trademark for the verb "photocopy" and noun "photocopier."

---

[8] Acetyl salicylic acid
[9] Moving stairway
[10] Rebound tumbling equipment
[11] Real estate trading game
[12] Solid carbon dioxide

POTENTIAL PROBLEMS IN THE
USE OF A TRADEMARK

In selecting a trademark to identify the particular goods or services of a
company, other factors should be considered in order to ensure that the
trademark is available for use and registration.

The basis of commerce in the United States, as in many other
countries, is that there is at least a minimum level of fair competition.
Trademark law is classified as being part of the broader spectrum of
law known as **unfair competition**.[13] In a free market society, it is
expected that a party would be prevented from gaining any advantage
by using marks that are similar to the marks already being used by
another party.

Trademark Infringement

Use of comparable or similar words or symbols that cause someone to
mistake the source of the goods sold under the mark causes confusion
in the public. This concept has become so essential to trademark law
that a party does not need to show that the public is actually confused
through the use of a similar mark.

Rather, all one needs to show is that there is a "likelihood of
confusion" in the minds of the public due to the similarity in the
respective goods or services of the parties. This is the legal test for
trademark infringement.

In determining whether there is a likelihood of confusion by the
purchasing public, we must analyze the similarity of the trademarks in
question themselves. Are they identical? Do they look similar, while
perhaps being spelled slightly differently? Is their pronunciation
similar? This is known as the "sight, sound, meaning trilogy."

---

[13] *Trademarks and Tradenames*, 74 Am.Jur. 2d § 84

Dilution

Dilution involves the use of a mark that blurs the distinctiveness of a famous mark or tarnishes the famous mark's reputation by using it in a disparaging manner. In determining whether a mark dilutes a famous mark, the goods or services of the respective parties need not be in competition or even related in some fashion.

For example, a paper recycling company that adopted the tag line "Just Do It" would diminish Nike's reputation in the mark for footwear. Although the public would not confuse the provider of the recycling services with the maker of shoes, the mark is so famous that it would be clear the recycling company is playing off Nike's reputation and the value that Nike had built up in the mark through extensive advertising.

Prior Registration

Trademarks may be registered at the state level in all fifty states, as well as at the United States Patent and Trademark Office. A **registration** is a recognition of a trademark owner's rights acquired through use of a mark. A trademark registration provides the owner with various legal presumptions regarding the extent of the owner's rights in the mark. For example, you might want to adopt and register the mark "HOT THINGS" for a line of clothing. If the Trademark Office had already registered "HOT THINGS" for shoes and socks, you would not be entitled to a registration, because there is a good chance that the consuming public would think that the company that distributes or manufactures the shoes and socks would also put out a line of clothing.

Prior Common Law Use of the Mark

Trademark rights in the United States are based on use, not on registration. A registration is essentially recognition by the federal government of a party's rights gained through use of a trademark in connection with particular goods or services created in the geographic area in which the mark has already been used and with sales, advertisements, and the distribution of promotional literature at tradeshows.

If no federal trademark registration exists, then different parties may possess valid common law rights in the identical mark for the identical products or services in different geographic areas.

Think of two small restaurants having the same name. One is in a small town in Texas, and the other is located in Washington state. The parties can expand their rights in the mark into other geographic areas of the United States as long as they do not encroach upon the other's territory. If the owner of the Washington state restaurant opened a restaurant under the same name in the same town as the Texas restaurant, then the Washington state business would infringe upon the Texas company.

Accordingly, the prior common law use of a trademark by another party may pose a potential problem if the territories conflict.

Term Is Generic

Following the logic of fair competition, trademark law is framed to protect society from losing the use of common, generic, terms in describing its goods or services. No one entity is entitled to use a word or phrase that is common to society. Terms such as "car," "pencil," and "restaurant" are basic terms that someone would need to identify these matters. No term that is wholly generic can be registered as a trademark in the United States.

As mentioned earlier, many trademarks have become generic through overuse and abuse of the mark.

Term Is Highly Descriptive

As discussed on page 39, merely descriptive marks are not considered "inherently distinctive" and are not entitled to protection or registration as a trademark when they are first used. Once the term has been extensively used and promoted, the public recognizes the term as the trademark of one party. The term is then protectable and registerable as a trademark because the mark has acquired secondary meaning.

A federal application to register the mark on the Principal Register will be denied if the descriptive mark has not acquired secondary meaning. The mark, however, may be registered on the Supplemental Register, which is a register of marks that are capable of becoming trademarks once there has been sufficient use to create the secondary meaning. A registration on the Supplemental Register, however, does not provide the owner with the same presumptions of ownership of the mark that a Principal Register registration does.

When selecting a new trademark, therefore, an owner should try to avoid the following categories, all of which are considered highly descriptive:

1.   Merely descriptive of the goods or services. For example, INTERACTIVE TOYS for computer games for children.

2.   Descriptively misdescriptive of the goods or services. For example, IRONSIDE for aluminum siding.

3.   Primarily geographically descriptive of the goods or services. For example, SANTA BARBARA HAMMERS, which describes the city in which the hammers are made.

4.   Primarily geographically deceptively misdescriptive of the goods or services. Terms that fall into this category are never capable of functioning as a trademark or being registerable, no matter how much the mark is used. For example, SHEFFIELD for stoves and ranges, because the mark falsely suggests a connection with the famous steel industry in Sheffield, England.

5.   Primarily merely a surname. A surname is a family name or last name. For example, JOHNSON or REYNOLDS are common surnames.

CHAPTER QUESTIONS

Trademark Basics

1.   What is a trademark, and what effect does a trademark have on the public?

2.   A person has asked you to help choose a new name for a computer. The person is torn between "PC PLUS" and "KIWI JR." What might you tell the person about these two choices?

3.   A client of your attorney wants to adopt the name "MYST" for a computer mouse. Do you think that the attorney may want to tell the client of any potential problems?

Chapter Five

THE U.S. TRADEMARK APPLICATION

ELEMENTS OF THE U.S. TRADEMARK APPLICATION

Section 1051(a) of the Lanham Act sets out the primary guidelines for the United States federal trademark application. These guidelines are expanded and detailed in the Trademark Manual of Examining Procedure (TMEP). The TMEP is published by the U.S. Patent and Trademark Office. Its purpose is to provide trademark examiners who are employed by the Trademark Office, applicants, and attorneys with a guide to the trademark practices and procedures of the Patent and Trademark Office. This section provides an overview of the preparation, filing and prosecution of a U.S. trademark application and the maintenance of the registration.

The Lanham Act provides for the following three separate bases for an applicant to register a mark:

1. use of a mark "in commerce"[1]
2. a foreign application or registrations owned by a qualified foreign applicant[2]
3. a bona fide intention to use the mark "in commerce" in connection with the goods or services identified in the application.[3]

In order for an application to be assigned a filing date, the application must include the following minimum elements:[4]

---

[1] 15 U.S.C. § 105(a)
[2] 15 U.S.C. § 1126(d) and (e)
[3] 15 U.S.C. § 1051(b)
[4] 37 C.F.R. § 2.21

> name of the applicant
> a name and address to which communications can be directed
> a drawing of the mark substantially meeting the requirements of 37 C.F.R. § 2.52 (Code of Federal Regulations)
> an identification of goods or services
> a claim of one of the three bases for filing
> a verification or declaration signed by the applicant
> the required filing fee.

A filing date will be assigned to an application only if all the necessary elements are filed together. This is critical, as the filing date of an application often becomes pivotal. It will give the application priority for consideration over other similar applications that may be filed later. Once the registration issues on the Principal Register, it provides constructive use of the mark as of the filing date, conferring certain rights of priority nationwide. There are, however, limitations to that priority. These limitations are found in Section 1057(c) of the Lanham Act.

Types of Applications

The trademark application must be filed in English in the United States. Applicants may use their own forms; however, all the elements required by law and found in the PTO form must be present in the application.

The applicant must verify the truth and accuracy of the information in the application and must sign the application. It is important to determine who should sign the application, using the following guidelines:

> If the applicant is an individual, that individual must sign.
> If the applicant is a partnership, a general partner must sign.
> If the applicant is a corporation, association or similar organization, an officer of the corporation, association or organization must sign. An officer is a person who holds an office established in the bylaws.
> If there are several parties who own the mark, each party must sign.

The person who signs the application must indicate the date signed, provide a telephone number to be used if it is necessary to contact the applicant, and clearly indicate a name and position.

Actual Use Applications

Prior to the revisions to the Lanham Act in 1988, all trademark applications needed to be based on actual use of the mark in interstate commerce. This generally meant that the applicant needed to assert that the mark was in use between at least two states or in use in a manner that was regulated by the federal government.

An application may still be based on actual use in commerce. If an application is filed based on actual use of the mark under Section 1051 of the Act, the applicant must state both the date of first use anywhere in the United States and the date when the mark was first used **in commerce.** Use of the mark in commerce refers to commerce that is regulated by the U.S. Congress. Such commerce includes:

1.   U.S. interstate commerce between two or more states
2.   commerce between a foreign country and the United States
3.   commerce between a U.S. territory and the United States
4.   commerce within the District of Colombia.

Actual use applications must include three specimens showing the use of the mark in commerce for the goods or services specified in the application. For goods, the specimens may be labels, tags or containers bearing the mark. For services, the specimens may be actual advertisements or promotional literature bearing the mark. Advertising agency mockups of advertisements or promotional literature are unacceptable.

Intent-To-Use Applications

Since 1989, it has been possible to file an application under Section 1051(b) of the Lanham Act to register a mark with the United States government based on a bona fide intention to use the mark in commerce in the future in connection with goods or services. The applicant must specify the manner in which he or she intends to use the mark in the future. The intention to use a mark must ultimately be perfected by filing a statement showing that use of the mark has commenced, along with a declaration verifying the dates of use.

Applications Based on a Foreign Registration or Application

Pursuant to various international treaties, an application in a foreign country may base a U.S. application on either a foreign application (if the U.S. application is filed within six months of the filing of the foreign application) or on a foreign registration.

If the U.S. application is based on a foreign application, then the U.S. application cannot be issued until a certified copy of the foreign registration is provided to the Trademark Office.

An application based on a foreign application or registration may also contain a separate claim that there is a bona fide intention to use the mark in commerce. In that way, the application may rely on the claim of intention to use if the foreign application never issues.

Concurrent Use Applications

Occasionally, a trademark owner will adopt a mark that is already being used by another trademark owner in another part of the United States. In these instances, assuming that the requirements of Section 1052(d) of the Act are met, the parties may agree to file applications that limit their registrations to certain geographic areas. For example, a drug store chain called "HEALTHY PEOPLE DRUG" may be established and well known in Washington, Oregon and California. Another company may be operating drug stores under the same mark in New York, Connecticut and Delaware. These two parties may agree to file applications that specifically exclude coverage in the other's established territories.

If the parties are not in agreement, then a concurrent use proceeding will be instituted by the Trademark Trial and Appeal Board in order to determine the territory each registration should cover. A concurrent use proceeding is similar to a litigation in court.

Supplemental Register

Applications are typically filed seeking registration on the Principal Register. As discussed in Chapter Four, if a mark is so highly descriptive that it is not inherently distinctive and the applicant cannot prove that the mark has acquired secondary meaning, then the mark may still be registerable on the Supplemental Register.

The Supplemental Register is defined as in Section 1091 as being a list of

> All marks capable of distinguishing applicant's goods
> or services and not registerable on the principal register
> herein provided, except those declared to be
> unregisterable ... which are in lawful use in commerce
> by the owner thereof, on or in connection with any
> goods or services may be registered on the
> supplemental register.

That is, these are marks that are not inherently distinctive, such as "TELEPHONE BOOKS PLUS" for yellow page directories, but are still capable of identifying a source for the goods and/or services. These marks must be in use at the time the decision is made to attempt to register on the Supplemental Register. There is no intent-to-use provision for the Supplemental Register.

Specification of Goods and Services

The specification, or identification, of goods or services is the statement by the applicant as to the scope of protection to be sought by the trademark application. It identifies the specific goods and services in connection with which the mark will be used. The Trademark Office uses the International Classification System (ICS) for categorizing the different types of goods and services for the purpose of registering a mark. The ICS is divided into 42 classes; 34 identify goods and the remaining eight identify services. A full list of the ICS may be found at Appendix Table 8.

Specification is a bit of a balancing act with the Trademark Office. The applicant would like to file as broadly within a specific class as possible, but the examiner wants to keep the specification narrow enough to allow sufficient room for competition. The allowable specifications change over the years.

As recently as 1994, the Trademark Office was accepting "telecommunication services in International Class 38" as an acceptable specification of services. This would, of course, offer a wide scope of protection. The telecommunications field is widely varied, covering traditional wireline, cellular and satellite communications. Currently, the Trademark Office is requiring that applicants narrow their specifications to indicate the type of telecommunication services such as "telephone communication services" or "cellular communication services."

Method of Use Clause

The applicant must state the method by which the mark is currently being used or intends to be used. If the statement is left out of the application, the application will not be considered complete. Often the applicant is offered the opportunity by the examining attorney to file an amendment adding the method-of-use clause, but this opportunity is at the discretion of the examiner.

The method-of-use clause sets forth how the mark is being or intends to be used in the trade. For example, if the application covers goods, then the method of use clause might state that the mark appears directly on the goods or their containers, while for services it might state that the mark appears in advertisements.

Power of Attorney

Individual applicants may represent themselves before the U.S. Trademark Office. Similarly, a corporation can name an individual officer to be its contact during examination of the application. Most applicants name an attorney to represent them. Any attorney admitted to the bar of any state within the United States may practice before the Trademark Office.

The power of attorney not only names a contact individual for the application, it also gives the address for the mailing of documents and a telephone number of the individual. When the name and address of an attorney appear in the papers, the Trademark Office will presume that the applicant wishes correspondence from the Trademark Office concerning the application to be sent to the attorney at that address.

Appointment of Domestic Representative

If an applicant is not a resident of the United States, the applicant must designate the name and address of a person who is resident in the United States to receive notices issued in proceedings affecting the mark. Usually, the attorney handling the application will also be designated as the applicant's domestic representative.

Drawing Sheet

A drawing sheet must always accompany a trademark application showing the mark sought to be registered, even if there is no design to the mark being filed. This sheet summarizes key elements of the application. It shows:

➢ the applicant's name and address
➢ the basis of use for filing (whether actual or intended)
➢ the specification of goods and/or services
➢ a graphic representation of the mark, which may be "typed," i.e., in block letters, depending on the circumstances
➢ the name, address and telephone number of the attorney or individual representing the applicant.

The drawing sheet exactly identifies the scope of the representation of the physical mark, much as the specification determines the scope of protection offered by the specification of goods and/or services. The eventual registration will protect the exact mark shown on the drawing sheet. The broadest protection is offered to marks that register in all block letters. Any addition of designs, stylizations or claiming of colors will limit the registration to that specific representation of the mark.

Specimens

As noted above, three specimens showing use of the mark may either
be submitted at the time of filing or during the prosecution of the
application (see below). Advertising mockups or fabricated specimens
of marks not in use will be rejected and may cause the rejection of the
application.

The Trademark Office prefers original specimens showing the use of
the mark. Photocopies of originals may be accepted. Bulky specimens
should not be submitted in their entirety; rather, representative sections
or pieces should be submitted. There is a chance that valuable
specimens, such as CDs, will be detached from the transmittal
documents and will become "lost" on their way to the examiner;
therefore, only photocopies of these valuable specimens should be
submitted.

If an original "valuable" specimen must be reviewed by the examiner,
an alternative is to arrange for the original specimen to be hand-
delivered to the examiner, a photocopy having already been previously
submitted.

THE LIFE OF A U.S. TRADEMARK APPLICATION

Initial Deadlines

The full cycle of a trademark application can often take between 13 and
24 months from the time of filing to a final decision on registration.
The process involves stages for review of the compliance of the
application with regulations, as well as examination of the application
for registerability.

The application is reviewed by an examiner at the Trademark Office,
and a dialog ensues over the months between the examiner and the
applicant, or the applicant's attorney.

Once the application is filed, the Trademark Office will review the
application to ensure all required elements of the application are

present. If the application is in order, the mailroom will assign a serial number, and the application will be forwarded to an examiner.

An Official Filing Receipt confirming the filing of the application and summarizing the main elements of the application will be prepared and sent to the applicant. This document will likely arrive within three months of filing. The applicant should review the document to ensure that all information, such as the representation of the mark, the description of goods and/or services, and the name of the applicant, appear correctly. If not, the applicant must submit a request to correct the information. It is the responsibility of the applicant to verify the accuracy of the data on the Official Filing Receipt.

Responses to Office Actions

Within a few months, the application is assigned to an examiner in the Trademark Office for review. The examining units are divided into different practice groups, or areas, that review applications along similar lines, such as a group that reviews software applications.

Frequently, the examiner will have a question about some element of the application or will not believe the mark is registerable as a trademark. In this instance, the examiner may try to resolve these issues by a telephone call to the applicant. Alternatively, the examiner may also choose to issue a formal statement of the objection or question. This document is called an **Office Action** or **Official Action**.

The applicant has a period of six months from the mailing date of the Office Action to respond to the issues raised by the examiner. If the applicant does not respond, the application will become abandoned. The application will also go abandoned if the applicant does not respond to all the issues raised by the examiner. Partial responses are considered to be nonresponsive. The six-month deadline is not extendable.

This cycle of Office Actions and responses can repeat as the applicant and the examiner try to resolve differences about the application. Typically, an examiner is allowed to address the same issue twice. If the issues cannot be resolved, the examiner will issue a Final Office

Action giving his or her final arguments to the applicant. The second Office Action is generally the "final" one. The applicant may then appeal the examiner's refusal of registration to the Trademark Trial and Appeal Board (TTAB), as explained below.

Amendments to Allege Use

If an application was filed on an intent-to-use basis, the application will not mature into a registration until use of the mark has commenced and evidence of such use is submitted to the Trademark Office. The application may be amended to include dates of use, if the use is begun during the time the examiner is reviewing the application.

If the examiner has completed the review of the application, then the application cannot be amended. Evidence of use must be submitted after the application is published for the purpose of opposition (see below). In that situation, a **Statement of Use** is filed.

The Amendment to Allege Use must include the dates of first use of the mark both anywhere and in interstate commerce. The document must include a declaration from the applicant verifying the accuracy of the dates. Three specimens showing the mark must be filed with the Amendment.

Publication

After the examiner has agreed that a trademark application may be registered on the Principal Register, the mark is published in the Patent and Trademark Office's (PTO) Official Gazette for the purpose of opposition by third parties. Marks that will register on the Supplemental Register are not published for the purpose of opposition. The Official Gazette is printed every Tuesday.

Appeals to TTAB

As mentioned above, the Trademark Trial and Appeal Board (TTAB) serves as the review body for the decisions of the examiners. The TTAB consists of nine members. In each case, a panel of three board members reviews the records of the application along with any supplemental briefs submitted by the applicant and Examiner. Before a ruling is issued, the applicant may request an oral argument before the panel.

Opposition Proceedings Filed by Third Parties

Publication of the mark constitutes public notice that the mark will soon register. This allows third parties to raise any objections to the mark if they feel it will somehow harm their right to do business. If a party feels that it will be harmed, it has the right to prevent registration by filing an opposition proceeding. The proceeding to oppose registration is argued before the TTAB. A successful opposition proceeding will only prevent the registration of a mark. The decision of the TTAB does not necessarily affect how the applicant will use the mark. Lawsuits to stop the use of a trademark must be filed and prosecuted through the state or, more usually, the federal court systems.

Postpublication Procedures

If the application was not opposed, or the application survives an opposition proceeding, then the application will proceed to the next step. An application falls into one of the following three categories:

1.   Applications where evidence of use has been filed.

       This category pertains to used-based applications or intent-to-use applications where an **Amendment to Allege Use** has been filed. In this situation, the certificate of registration will issue in due course.

2.   Applications where a foreign certificate of registration has been filed.

       This category pertains only to applications filed under Section 44(d) of the Lanham Act that are based on foreign applications. In order for the U.S. application to register, a certified copy of the foreign registration must be filed with the Trademark Office. If this has been done, then the registration certificate will issue in due course.

3.   **Intent-to-Use applications** where evidence of use has not been
        filed.

        The category pertains only to intent-to-use applications where
        an Amendment to Allege Use was not filed during the
        prosecution before publication. The Trademark Office will
        issue a Notice of Allowance, and the application will have six
        months from the mailing date of the Notice to file a Statement
        of Use or to file a Request for an Extension of Time to file the
        Statement.

If use of the mark has not commenced prior to the six-month deadline,
the extension required may be filed, explaining that the applicant still
has a bona fide intention to use the mark along with the filing fee. The
applicant may extend the deadline for filing the Statement of Use for a
maximum of 36 months from the mailing date of the Notice of
Allowance. Extension requests must be filed every six months.

If a Statement of Use is filed and accepted by the Trademark Office, a
certificate of registration will issue in due course.

Changes of Title

A trademark and its registration will often be transferred to another
party, or the company will simply change its corporate name. A
registered trademark is property with value for the trademark owner.
To record the change, a document showing the transfer (such as an
assignment or change of name), along with an official cover sheet, is
recorded at the Assignment Branch of the Patent and Trademark
Office. This office is still a joint office for both patent and trademark
records. A recordation fee is set forth in the Code of Federal
Regulations. Once the assignment is recorded by the Assignment
Branch, the change of title becomes part of the trademark's official
record.

POST-REGISTRATION MATTERS

Filing Section 8 & 15 Affidavits

A trademark registration is not valid indefinitely. Currently, a registration is valid for a period of 10 years, with maintenance required between the fifth and sixth years of registration. By the sixth year of registration, the owner of the registration must file an affidavit declaring that the mark is still in use in commerce in connection with the goods or services covered by the registration and attach a specimen showing current use. This is known as an Affidavit Under Section 8. The failure to file this Affidavit will result in the cancellation of the registration by the PTO.

In order for the registration to become "incontestable," the registration may also submit an Affidavit Under Section 15 if the following conditions are met:

1.   The mark has been in continuous use in commerce for five consecutive years subsequent to the date of registration in connection with the goods or services specified in the registration.

2.   There has been no final decision adverse to the registrant's claim of ownership in the mark.

3.   There is no proceeding involving the registrant's rights in the mark pending in the PTO or in a court.

Once the registration becomes "incontestable" by the filing of the Affidavit Under Section 15, the bases for cancellation of the registration become limited.

The Affidavits Under Sections 8 and 15 cannot be executed until the fifth anniversary of the date of registration.

Renewal of Registrations

Trademark registrations may have an indefinite life as long as they are
renewed at the end of each term valid registration. Currently, the term
of registration is 10 years. An applicant must submit a renewal
application declaring that the mark is still in use in commerce in
connection with the goods or services specified in the registrations by
the owner of the registration. An appropriate specimen showing current
use of the mark in connection with the goods or services must
accompany the renewal application, together with a filing fee.

The renewal application may not be executed until six months prior to
the tenth anniversary of the date of registration. If the renewal
application is accepted, the registration will remain in force for another
10 years, at which time it may be renewed again. The renewal
application may be filed within the three-month grace period that
follows the renewal deadline.

Cancellation of Registrations

A petition to cancel a registration may be filed by persons who believe
that they are or will be damaged by the registration of the mark.
Cancellation proceedings are held before the TTAB. If the third party is
successful, the registration will be cancelled and removed from the
federal register.

TRADEMARK NOTICE SYMBOLS

Protecting a trademark begins with letting people know the mark is a
trademark. This is accomplished simply by using the following symbols
to the right of the trademark, when appropriate:

> ® – the encircled "R" symbol indicates that a trademark is
> registered at the Trademark Office on either the Principal or
> Supplemental Registers in connection with the goods and/or
> services recited in the registration. This symbol should not be
> used in connection with a mark that is the subject of a pending
> application.

™ – This symbol may be used in connection with any mark that identifies a product. This symbol merely indicates that a person is claiming rights in a trademark, irrespective of whether the trademark is the subject of a pending application at the Trademark Office or at the state level.

ˢᴹ – This symbol may be used in connection with a mark that identifies services. This symbol merely indicates that a person is claiming rights in a service mark, irrespective of whether the trademark is the subject of a pending application at the Trademark Office or at the state level.

The symbols do not have to appear every time the mark is used in one item.

CHAPTER QUESTIONS

The U.S. Trademark Application

1.   What are the different types of trademark applications in the United States? How does the question of use of the mark affect the type of application to be filed?

2.   Explain the typical life cycle of a United States trademark application. How does the question of use of the mark affect its life cycle?

3.   It is between the fifth and sixth year of registration for the mark of one of your clients. Your client has told you that although it stopped using the mark three years ago, it has just re-introduced the product to the market. Can you file any documentation to preserve the original registration, or is it necessary to file a new application with the new dates of use?

Chapter Six

THE INTERNATIONAL
TRADEMARK APPLICATION

THE MYTH OF THE UNIVERSAL
TRADEMARK REGISTRATION

A frequent assumption among trademark owners in the United States is
that their registrations are valid throughout the world. Trademark law
and protection arise on a national basis. As a general rule, registration
covers only one country, and separate applications have to be made in
each country where one intends to use and protect a mark.

Registrations in the United States (with the exception of concurrent use
registrations[1]) give the owner protection in all 50 states and the United
States territories. Currently, there is no universal trademark
registration.

Numerous international treaties exist that provide for the protection and
registration of trademarks. In addition, the United States has entered
into bilateral treaties with various countries regarding the protection of
trademarks.

The Madrid Agreements

The World Intellectual Property Organization (WIPO) does, however,
maintain an International Register that allows certain countries to obtain
a multinational registration. This practice was instituted with The
Madrid Agreement Concerning the International Registration of Marks
(the "Madrid Agreement"), signed in 1891.

Under the Madrid Agreement, once a trademark owner in a member
nation obtains a registration in the home nation, a Madrid Agreement
application may be filed with WIPO. Thus, the Madrid Agreement

---

[1] See Chapter Four

offers trademark registration in various countries through a single application. The registration is commonly referred to as an **international registration.**

A home nation trademark registration serves in the WIPO application as the basis for an international application. However, if the home national registration is cancelled within the first five years after registration, then the international registration will also be cancelled.

It is because of this "central attack" provision, along with some other provisions, that a number of countries, including the United States, did not join the Madrid Agreement. Other countries that are not members include Canada, Denmark, Greece, India, Ireland, Japan, Taiwan, and the United Kingdom.

A Protocol to the Madrid Arrangement the ("Madrid Protocol") was adopted in 1989. The Madrid Protocol provides for the filing of international applications at the same time as the filing for the home national application. It provides for the conversion of an international application into a national application if the home registration fails within the first five years. Although initially the U.S. was expected to join the Madrid Protocol, the U.S. has recently indicated that it will not join.

The Paris Convention

The Paris Convention for the Protection of Industrial Property, signed in 1883, as revised July 14, 1967, (the "Paris Convention"), addresses various forms of **industrial property.** Article 1(2) of the Paris Convention defines "industrial property" as including "trademarks, appellations, patents, utility models, industrial designs, and unfair competition." More than 110 countries, including the United States, are members of this treaty, which is also administered by WIPO.

Among other requirements, the Paris Convention obligates member nations to recognize a "priority filing date" of an application that is first filed in a home country for the applicant that is another member country. That is, a signatory to the Paris Convention will give the same home filing date to a trademark application filed in foreign countries, provided that the applicant files the foreign application within six months of the home ("priority") application filing.

Regional Treaties

Certain limited cooperative trademark registries do, however, exist. One such multination registry is the Organization Africaine de la Propriété Intellectuelle or the African Intellectual Property Organization, known as the AIPO. This is a common registry for many of the French-speaking coastal countries in Africa. The member countries of the AIPO are Benin, Burkina Faso, Cameroon, Central African Republic, Chad, Congo, Gabon, Guinea, Ivory Coast, Mali, Mauritania, Niger, Senegal, and Togo. A registration in one member country is automatically valid in all member countries.

On March 6, 1997, the Banjul Protocol came into effect and created another multination registry for trademarks. This registry is known as the ARIPO (African Regional Industrial Property Organization). The ARIPO is composed primarily of English-speaking African countries. The member countries are Botswana, Gambia, Ghana, Kenya, Lesotho, Malawi, Sierra Leone, Somalia, Sudan, Swaziland, Tanzania, Uganda, Zambia and Zimbabwe. Prior to 1997, the ARIPO only accepted multi-national patent filings.

Another multination registry is known as Benelux. This registry is in force for the countries of Belgium, Luxembourg and the Netherlands. The trademark office for the registry is located in The Hague in the Netherlands.

THE COMMUNITY TRADEMARK

On April 1, 1996, it became possible to obtain one trademark registration throughout the entire European Union. The European Union presently covers Austria, Belgium, Denmark, England, Finland, France, Germany, Greece, Ireland, Italy, Luxembourg, Netherlands, Portugal, Spain, and Sweden.

The so-called community trademark may be obtained by filing an application with the Office for Harmonization in the Internal Market

("OHIM") in Alicante, Spain, or in a national trademark registrar in a member state. If a trademark is unregisterable in any of the countries of the Union, then the application will be rejected for the entire Union.

The application may be filed in any one of the official languages of the European Union, but must designate one of the five official languages of the OHIM. The official languages are Spanish, German, English, French, and Italian. An applicant may also claim the priority of an issued registration in any of the member countries. Unlike the Madrid Protocol, a trademark owner does not need to be a national of a member country.

The community trademark will offer protection in each and every country of the European Union. Third parties may file oppositions against the community trademark application. It is important for the opposer to note that the unsuccessful party in the proceedings pays the costs, up to a maximum limit, of the party who prevails in the action. The OHIM allows for a short period after the filing of an opposition in which an application may be withdrawn without the penalty of paying the fees and costs of the other party.

If the community trademark application or registration is lost, a trademark owner may convert the application by filing corresponding national applications, and the applicant will be allowed to maintain the original community trademark filing date.

INTERNATIONAL TRADEMARK FILING CONSIDERATIONS

Mark Often Not a Requirement

Unlike the United States, use of a mark is very often not a requirement for obtaining a registration. This allows many trademark owners to obtain protection in countries where use has not actually begun or is not expected to begin for several years.

Therefore, many countries give priority to a trademark owner who is the **first to file** an application. Other countries give priority to a trademark owner who is the **first to register** the mark. A first-to-file country will register the first application filed regardless of the rights another trademark owner may have in the mark through use. A first-to-register country will take in account other factors, such as prior rights, piracy or fraud, or the form of a mark before granting registration.

It is important to remember that the majority of the countries do have a prescribed time in which use of the mark is required to commence for the registration to be enforceable. The individual trademark registries will not cancel the registration for nonuse within the different periods; however, a third party may petition to have the registration removed based on such nonuse.

The community trademark is different from the other international registries in that it *does* require use to maintain the registration. Proof of use must be filed with the OHIM within the first five years of registration. The use may be made in any one of the member countries.

Trademark Piracy

In order to protect their rights, owners of trademarks having business or prospective business in foreign countries who desire to protect their marks in such countries should ascertain the nature of the trademark laws in those countries. In many foreign countries a resident may obtain a registration of a trademark without having actually used it in trade. Such a registration may be used to prevent the importation into that country of goods bearing the mark.

International Translation of Marks

Differences in languages may lead to difficulties when the trademark owner begins to file in countries outside the United States. The mark may have a negative or derogatory meaning in the language of another country. Chevrolet discovered to its distress that its "Nova" mark meant "no go" ("no va") in the Spanish-speaking countries. Also, while the mark "Impreso" for printed paper products might be protectable in the United States, the term "Impreso" means "printed paper" in Spanish and is, therefore, generic in Spanish-speaking countries.

Some trademark owners try to find words that have little or no meaning in as many countries as possible. The most successful of these types of arbitrary marks is "Exxon," which was designed not to have any meaning in any language.

THE LIFE OF AN INTERNATIONAL TRADEMARK APPLICATION

Initial Deadlines

The lifecycles of trademarks in countries outside the United States may vary dramatically. Applications filed in Aruba will issue into a registration the same day, while applications filed in Japan, Argentina, Italy or Saudi Arabia may take up to 10 years to issue.

Powers of Attorney and Related Documents

In general, applications in foreign jurisdictions will require that certain documents be filed to allow prosecution of the application. These include powers of attorney for the foreign attorney or trademark agent ("foreign associate"), statements of incorporation or business, and (under certain circumstances) copies of earlier filed applications of the mark in other countries.

Most countries will allow the late filing of documents, but some will require that these be submitted along with the new application.

The most commonly requested document is the power of attorney for the foreign associate. This document allows the associate to represent the trademark owner before the trademark office in a specific country. These powers ask for the name and address of the trademark owner and may require a brief statement about the business or nature of the owner. It is best to rely on the forms supplied by the foreign associate to ensure that all the requirements are met. The filing of any documents in foreign jurisdictions requires that the documents be recognized and verified as authentic. This may require that the documents be legalized.[2]

---

[2] For full comments on legalization, please see Chapter Eleven

If the country belongs to the 1961 Hague Convention Abolishing the Requirement of Legalization for Foreign Public Documents, then no legalization will be required. Rather, the document may simply be signed by a representative of the trademark owner without notarization. If notarization of a document is required for a Hague Convention country, then only a simple document called an **apostille** issued by the Notary Commission of a state will need to be attached.

Responses

It is difficult to judge the time frame required for responses in foreign jurisdictions. Some foreign agents will require an immediate answer or an answer within a few days. Others, such as New Zealand, will give the trademark owner a full year to respond.

Unlike the United States, Office Actions and deadlines are not easily recognized in a foreign country. As the Office Action will be issued in the national language the foreign associate will usually write a letter to the trademark owner. It is important to read each letter carefully to understand what the associate is communicating from the local trademark office.

A response letter should be sent as far in advance of the deadline as possible to allow the associate time to translate the instructions and prepare the response. It is possible that, if the trademark associate is in a different time zone, the associate may begin the deadline day well ahead of the trademark owner.

Registered User or License Agreements

Trademark owners will often authorize another party to use the mark in a foreign country. This license agreement may need to be registered with the foreign trademark office. The trademark owner could lose the benefits of both the use of the mark and the registration if the license is not recorded as required.

A separate document called a **registered user application** may also be required. This will allow the other party's use of the mark to be recognized by the government of that country for purposes of protection and enforcement of rights. The foreign agent will inform the trademark owner if any third party documents are required.

Issuance of Registration

Once the registration certificate issues, the trademark owner may use the appropriate registration symbol next to the mark. Some countries, such as Mexico, require the use of a registration symbol with a mark. The term limits vary for the length of the registration. Usually the term is 10 years, as in the United States. Some countries, such as the Bahamas, follow the old British registration system. This means that the registration is valid for seven years and renewable each 14 years after the first renewal.

POSTISSUANCE MATTERS

Meeting Use Requirements

Having secured registration, the trademark owner often does not think about the mark in the various countries until it is time for renewal. This is because the vast majority of countries do not require filing any evidence of use before or after the registration issues in order to maintain the registration.

Some countries require that evidence of use be submitted during the first few years of registration and at certain intervals after the first filing. The trademark offices do not actively cancel registrations without use statements; however, these registrations become vulnerable to cancellation by third parties. Without use, the registrations usually do not survive cancellation actions.

Renewal of Registrations

As mentioned above, registrations are renewed on different schedules depending on the country. The renewal applications, like the original applications, are prepared and filed by the foreign associates. A new power of attorney may be required.

The renewal process is often seamless. Some countries, such as Japan, may require that evidence of use be filed at the time of renewal. If the trademark owner has not made use of the mark during the prescribed time, then a new application for a new registration should be filed to protect the mark.

A PARALEGAL'S ROLE IN INTERNATIONAL TRADEMARK PROSECUTION

Research Country Law and Requirements

The paralegal is valuable in the prosecution and maintenance of foreign trademarks applications and registrations. Much of the preliminary research on the filing and maintenance requirements may be prepared by the paralegal for the attorney's review.

Care should be taken to research each country individually. Generalizations, such as the ones in this book, will not allow the paralegal to understand the specific requirements for each country. This understanding comes through experience and research in available reference materials.

Liaison Between Foreign Agent and U.S. Attorney

The paralegal can also take the initiative to ensure that all the information is communicated effectively between the foreign agent and the attorney. When a letter is received from a foreign agent, the paralegal should look for deadlines in the letter and gather any relevant country information for the attorney's review.

Similarly, the paralegal should ensure that the attorney's responses and comments are communicated to the agent in a timely and clear manner. Also, the paralegal should follow up with a note to check that the agent has received the information and has acted on the information. The fax machine in the associate's office may be out of order, or a delivery may not arrive. A note to check in advance of the deadline will help ensure that no applications are lost due to a lack of communication between the attorney and the associate.

Liaison Between Client and Attorney

In the same way, the paralegal can follow up on requests for information from the client, the trademark owner, in advance of deadlines. This follow-through can minimize or eliminate any misunderstandings or miscommunications between the attorney and the client. Many times the paralegal is more accessible than the attorney.

Preparation of Documents for Filing

The research and liaison work will provide the necessary information and requirements. The paralegal will take the responsibility of preparing the documents for filing in accordance with country laws and treaties. Paralegals become integral in the prosecution and maintenance of foreign trademark applications and registrations by taking the initiative to manage the foreign filing programs.

CHAPTER QUESTIONS

The International Trademark Application

1.   How does the Paris Convention affect filings in foreign countries?

2.   Does the community trademark application differ from any of the other multinational registration applications?

3.   How does the question of the use of the mark affect applications in different foreign countries?

4.   A letter has come in from a foreign associate telling you of a two-week deadline for responding to a problem raised by the trademark office in that country. As a paralegal, what steps would you take?

EXERCISES

A.   Compose memos recommending a course of action for you and your attorney concerning the following fact patterns. Be certain to address questions about forms and procedures needed, as well as the research tools (refer to Appendix Tables 1 and 2) needed to accomplish each project.

1.   An owner of a pet shop located on Main and Elm wants to register the name of the business, "MAIN & ELM STREET PET STORE."

2.   A doll importer has developed the name of "MR. ALONZO'S FINDS." The dolls are imported from Switzerland, Germany and Thailand and are distributed throughout the United States. He would like to protect the name in as many countries as would seem reasonable for his work. For the sake of this exercise, assume that the mark is clear and available for use.

B.   Using the forms supplied by the United States Trademark Office, complete an application to register a mark under the following conditions:

1.   The mark is ZEBRA STRIPES.
2.   The mark will be used on running shoes and for the name of a shoe store.
3.   The mark is not in use but the owner plans to use it within a year.
4.   The owner is Zebra Stripes Corporation, a Delaware Corporation, located and doing business at 1212 Main Place, Anytown USA, 11122.
5.   Mr. Raymond Smith is the president of Zebra Stripes Corporation.
6.   Mr. Smith wants your attorney to act on his behalf. You can create the identity of your attorney if necessary.
7.   Zebra Stripes Corporation has a sister company in Germany called Tiger Stripes, GmbH who will first ship the shoes to the United States.

Chapter Seven

COPYRIGHT BASICS

COPYRIGHT LAW IN GENERAL

The first United States Copyright Act was enacted in 1790 and was entitled "An Act for the Encouragement of Learning, by Securing the Copies of Maps, Charts and Books, to the Authors and Proprietors of such Copies, during the Times therein Mentioned." The current copyright law in the United States was enacted in 1976.[1]

Copyright law protects the expression of an idea. It does not protect the idea itself. The copyright laws extend protection to

"... original works of authorship fixed in any tangible medium of expression, now known or later developed, from which they can be perceived, reproduced, or otherwise communicated, either directly or with the aid of a machine or device. Works of authorship include the following categories:

> literary works
> musical works, including any accompanying words
> dramatic works, including any accompanying music, pantomimes and choreographic works
> pictorial, graphic, and sculptural works
> motion pictures and other audiovisual works
> sound recordings
> architectural works." [2]

The copyright in an item exists from the moment of creation.[3] The copyright in the work immediately becomes the property of the author who created it. Much like the term of a patent, the term of a copyright

---

[1] 17 U.S.C. §§ 101-1010
[2] 17 U.S.C. § 102
[3] 17 U.S.C. § 302

is fixed by law. After a copyright expires, the copyrighted material will pass into the public domain and is available for use by anyone.

The duration of a copyright depends in large part on when the work in question was created. Whether or not the work was created before January 1, 1978, could substantially effect the lifespan of the copyright.

In order to determine the duration of the copyright in a work created before January 1, 1978, refer to Sections 302, 303 and 304 of the Act. The term of the copyright must be carefully calculated depending upon the factors such as whether the work was published or registered for copyright, whether the copyright was in its first term on January 1, 1978, and whether the copyright was in its renewal term before January 1, 1978.

In any work created on or after January 1, 1978, for which the copyright is owned by an individual, the copyright will last for the life of the author, plus an additional 50 years. For works created after 1978 where the copyright is owned by an employer of the author as a **work made for hire,** the copyright will last 75 years from the date of publication, or 100 years from the date of creation, whichever occurs first.

Works that are owned by the employer are known as "works made for hire."

Unless there is an agreement to the contrary, the authors of a joint work are co-owners of the copyright in the work. The U.S. Act specifies materials that are not subject to copyright protection. These include ideas (discussed below), facts, titles, names, short phrases, and blank forms.

Copyrighted works pass into the public domain after the copyright either expires or is lost. While it is extremely difficult to lose copyright protection under today's laws, this has not been the case in the past.

For example, all works first published before January 1, 1978, that did not contain a valid copyright notice may be considered to be in the public domain. Owners of works published between January 1, 1978, and prior to March 1, 1989, that did not contain a valid copyright notice were given a five-year grace period in which to correct the problem of publication without notice before their work became part of the **public domain**.[4]

As a practical note, the public domain contains all works for which the statutory copyright period has expired. Consequently, the public is free to copy any work that is in the public domain and all works that were never protectable by copyright laws.

United States government documents and publications are not deemed under the law to be entitled to copyright protection and, therefore, are considered to be in the public domain. These works must have been authored by employees of the federal government, as opposed to any of its contractors.

Finally, works may enter the public domain if the copyright owner specifically grants and donates the work to the public domain.

STATUTORY ELEMENTS OF COPYRIGHTABLE SUBJECT MATTER

For a work to be considered protectable under copyright, it must meet relatively minimal standards.

Originality

The term **original** in the context of U.S. copyright law means only that the work has its origin or beginning with the author. Unlike patent and trademark law, there is no requirement that a copyrighted work be different and unique from everything that has come before the creation of the work.

Rather, the copyrightable work only needs to embody a minimum level of creativity. The work must have originated with the author claiming copyright. This is why several novels with the same general plot may

---

[4] See the Copyright Office's Circular 1 - *Notice of Copyright*

be copyrighted. It is the original expression of the idea that is the subject of the copyright, not the idea itself.[5]

Fixation

To receive copyright, the work must be "fixed" in a tangible medium of expression. Simply put, any stable medium or format from which the work can be read back or heard, either directly or with the aid of a machine or device, is acceptable for copyright protection.

For example, a work is protected when it is written or drawn on a piece of paper, typed on a typewriter, or recorded on tape. A performance is fixed if it is recorded on videotape or photographed.

Computer software satisfies the fixation requirement the moment it is stored on magnetic media such as disks or tapes, imprinted on devices such as chips and circuit boards, or written down on paper. A computer display is considered to be fixed even if it was held in memory for a few seconds during a display.[6]

WHEN ORIGINALITY IS NOT ORIGINAL

Derivative Works

Copyright owners have the exclusive right to reproduce the copyrighted work, to prepare derivative works based on the copyrighted work, to distribute copies to the public by sale, rental or lease, the right to perform the work in public, and the right to display the work in public.[7]

For example, an author can receive copyright protection for a book that describes a scientific method. But this protection extends only to the unique expression of the method in the book, not to the actual method described. The public is free to follow the method or use the scientific

---

[5] *Feist Publications, Inc. v. Rural Telephone Service Company, Inc.*, 111 S.Ct 1282, 1287-88 (1991)

[6] *Mai v. Peak*, 991 F.2d. 511 (9th Cir. 1993)

[7] 17 U.S.C. § 106

information in the book without risk of infringing upon the author's copyright.

Any work that contains an editorial revision, annotation or explanation is considered a derivative work; however, the work of the creator of the derivative work must be more than a trivial change in the first work. It is also important to remember that the creator of the original work has the "exclusive" right to make derivative works.

For example, Puccini's opera *Madame Butterfly* was copyrighted in 1914. This opera was based on Belasco's 1909 play that was, in turn, based on Long's 1897 novel. Each was created with the permission of the prior copyright owner. Each version had separate, new copyrightable matter, but this new copyright did not extend to the previously copyrighted matter by the prior owner.[8]

If an author has adapted or recast another, preexisting work, such as making a translation, arrangement or dramatization with the copyright owner's permission, if needed,[9] then the unique expression contributed by the second author is copyrightable as a separate work.

While a translator could provide a Spanish or French version of a Shakespearean play, which could be separately copyrighted, others would be free to make their own Spanish translations of Shakespeare. They must not, however, copy any previous copyrighted translation.

Fair Use

There are certain limits to the copyright owner's exclusive rights in a work. One of the most important exceptions to a copyright owner's rights is the public's right to make **fair use**[10] of a copyrighted work. Fair use is a limited use of a copyrighted work without the copyright owner's permission. Fair use does not involve any liability for infringement.

---

[8] *G. Ricordi & Co. v. Paramount Pictures, Inc.*, 189 F.2d 469 (2d. Cir. 1951)
[9] No permission would be needed if the original work was either in the public domain or was a primarily a compilation of facts and figures.
[10] 17 U.S.C. § 107

Fair use includes the use of a copyrighted work for purposes such as criticism, comment, parody, news reporting, teaching, scholarship or research. Although the fair use provision has been around since the *Sony v. Betamax* case came before the Supreme Court in 1984 and was included in the Copyright Act prior to the 1990s, it was again brought into the forefront of copyright law by the case of 2 Live Crew.[11]

In brief, in 1964 Roy Orbison and William Dees wrote the song "Oh, Pretty Woman" and assigned their rights in it to Acuff-Rose Music, Inc. Acuff-Rose then registered the song for copyright protection. On July 5, 1989, the manager of the rap group 2 Live Crew informed Acuff-Rose that the group had written a parody of "Oh, Pretty Woman," and asked for permission to record the parody.

Acuff-Rose refused permission but, nevertheless, in 1989, 2 Live Crew released its version of "Oh Pretty Woman" on records, cassette tapes, and compact discs. The courts, including the Supreme Court, held that 2 Live Crew's parody was a fair use of the original Orbison version.

The 2 Live Crew case held the following four factors to be considered in determining whether or not a work qualifies for protection under the concept of fair use:

1.   One considers the purpose and character of use, including the commercial nature or nonprofit educational purposes, the reasons for the use such as criticism, teaching, or research and the amount of change from the original work.

2.   One looks at the nature of the original copyrighted work to determine how much copyright protection can be given to the original work. If the original work was a compilation of figures or contains many unoriginal elements itself, protection may be limited.

3.   One considers the relative amount of the original work in the subsequent work. The second author must take no more than

---

[11] *Campbell v. Acuff-Rose Music*, 114 S.Ct. 1164 (1994)

would be necessary from the original work and cannot take the most definitive part of the work.

4.   One considers the extent of harm to the market or potential market of the original work caused by the infringement. This test takes into account harm to the original, as well as harm to any legitimate derivative works.

Consideration of all these factors determines whether a use of a previously copyrighted work is a fair use. It usually does not become a consideration until the second use becomes financially successful. 2 Live Crew's recording sold over half a million copies before Acuff-Rose brought the initial lawsuit.

BARS TO COPYRIGHT PROTECTION

Ideas

Ideas, as explained above, are not protectable in and of themselves by copyright law. Section 102 (b) states that

> In no case does copyright protection for an original
> work of authorship extend to any idea, procedure,
> process, system, method of operation, concept,
> principle, or discovery, regardless of the form in which
> it is described, explained, illustrated, or embodied in
> such work.

Thus, no idea, only the expressions of the idea, may be held proprietary under copyright law. If an idea has value, such value would be the subject of a patent, not copyright, application.

Facts and Titles

Preexisting factual information and data are not protectable in and of themselves. Rather, it is the arrangement or compilation of the data that may be protectable under the copyright.[12] For example, no one cannot

---

[12] 17 U.S.C. § 101

copyright the subject matter of a calendar. The days of the week and the months of the year are available to everyone. The expression of those days and weeks, however, may be copyrightable works.

Mere titles of works, as well as names, short phrases, and slogans are not copyrightable. If these types of property have value, then they may be protectable under other theories of intellectual property protection, such as the law of trademarks. Symbols or designs, mere variations of typographic ornamentation, lettering, or coloring and mere listings of ingredients, or contents are not copyrightable. Each different *expression* of these elements may, however, be the subject of a copyright.

OWNERSHIP OF COPYRIGHT

Copyright is vested "in the author of the work."[13] Any individual who actually creates the work is the **author** of the work. The copyright in the work of authorship immediately becomes the property of the author who created it. Only the author or those deriving their rights through the author can rightfully claim copyright.

Determination of authorship is relatively simple when only one individual is involved in the creation of the work. However, there are a number of situations that complicate the question of authorship.

Works for Hire

In a work made for hire, the employer of the author is considered to be the actual author and not the creating individual. 17 U.S.C. § 101 defines a "work made for hire" as:

> (1) a work prepared by an employee within the scope of his or her employment; or

> (2) a work specially ordered or commissioned for use as a contribution to a collective work, as a part of a motion picture or other audiovisual work, as a translation, as a

---

[13] 17 U.S.C. § 201(a)

supplementary work, as a compilation, as an instructional text, as a test, as answer material for a test, or as an atlas, if the parties expressly agree in a written instrument signed by them that the work shall be considered a work made for hire....

This situation is different from a simple transfer of ownership of a copyright. In a transfer situation, the new party, not the author, becomes the owner of the work. A work-for-hire transfer may be terminated after 35 years if the transfer was acquired through actual assignment of the work.

Under a work for hire, the employer is considered to be the owner. This is significant, because the copyright duration for a work for hire is 75 years from the publication date or 100 years from its creation, whichever occurs first, rather than being based on the life of the author.[14]

Joint Works

A piece is defined as a **joint work** when two or more authors make original contributions of authorship "with the intention that their contributions be merged into inseparable or interdependent parts of a unitary whole."[15]

For example, joint works are created when two computer programmers work together to create the source code and user interface for a single program or when a lyricist and a composer collaborate on a single song.

In the first example, the two contributions would be "inseparable" because each piece could not work without the other. The song collaboration illustrates works that are "interdependent"; that is, they can be separated, but rely on each other for this one expression of the song.

---

[14] 17 U.S.C. § 302(c)
[15] 17 U.S.C. § 101

Derivative Works and Contributions

A **derivative work** is one in which the original author has given his or her consent to the creation of another similar work based on the original expression. Contributions are also created with the consent of the original author. Rather than being another expression of the original, a **contribution** is an enhancement to the original work, such as a new chapter or editorial comments in a book or a new verse to a song.

The right to allow derivative works or contributions may change significantly if the ownership is transferred or if the copyright is not renewed. If a copyright is not renewed, then the work passes into the public domain and no permission is required. However, if the ownership is transferred, the new owner may not permit any derivation or contribution even if the right was granted by the previous owner. The current owner has the right to control the use of the work.

Collective Works

Collective works are works that are composed of separate individual works, such as a collection of poems or songs or an issue of a magazine. Copyright in each separate contribution to a collective work is distinct from copyright in the collective work as a whole and remains with the author of the contribution. Therefore, while the publisher or collector may own the copyright in the entire collective work, the individual contributors retain the copyrights in their original contributions to the collective work. Licensing or transfer of collective works will require the permission of all the authors involved.

Compulsory Licenses

A **compulsory license** is a grant to use some form of intellectual property through a means set up by the government for a public interest. In general, United States intellectual property law does not allow for the concept of a compulsory license. However, the current Act of 1976 allows for five compulsory licenses:

1.   cable television transmissions[16]
2.   phonographic recordings[17]
3.   jukeboxes[18]
4.   noncommercial broadcasting[19]
5.   satellite transmissions.[20]

A compulsory license means that the owner of the copyright is obligated to grant requesting individuals the right to use their works for a set fee. For example, a songwriter may not control which music stores carry the album or which television stations broadcast the music video. In turn, under a compulsory license the artist receives royalties for each use of the work. Section 801 of the Act established the Copyright Royalty Tribunal, which sets the rates for the compulsory licenses, collects the fees, and distributes the money to the copyright owners.

The question of licensing, compulsory, or otherwise, has become complicated by the age of the Internet. Enforcement of one's own copyright has become very tenuous and uncertain.

Images, messages, and even the text of entire sites posted on the World Wide Web can be copied and incorporated into documents. With this in mind, many operators of websites have requested that their authors sign documents acknowledging this fact and, in practice, granting a compulsory license to their work by having it posted on the Internet.

The actual enforcement of the rights of the copyright owners and any implied or compulsory licenses on the Internet is being redefined daily. This is occurring on both a national and international level. Currently, for example, many companies are requiring that the authors sign export control agreements or acknowledgments before posting their information to the global electronic community.

---

[16] 17 U.S.C. § 111
[17] 17 U.S.C. § 115
[18] 17 U.S.C. § 116
[19] 17 U.S.C. § 118
[20] 17 U.S.C. § 119

CHAPTER QUESTIONS

Copyright Basics

1.   Someone asks you if he can copyright an idea that he has had. How would you respond?

2.   Can anything that is not original be protected under copyright?

3.   Explain the different types of ownership of a copyright. Is there a form that is not owned by the author?

Chapter Eight

THE COPYRIGHT APPLICATION

By Christine Wilson
Thomson & Thomson
Washington Services

COPYRIGHT FILING

Filing a copyright registration is a relatively simple process involving filling out a simple form and submitting it to the U.S. Copyright Office along with a fee. Currently the filing fee is $20.

The Forms

The Copyright Office has forms that cover all possible works that are submitted. There are forms covering:

> ➤ performing arts (screenplays, motion pictures, plays)
> ➤ visual arts (photographs, drawings)
> ➤ textual works (books)
> ➤ sound recordings
> ➤ software programs.

Following is a description of the forms currently used by the United States Copyright Office. The Copyright Office uses recognizable initials to identify the type of work the form is designed to represent.

PA – Referring to protection for the **performing arts**, this form is used for registering published or unpublished works in that area. These are works that are performed directly or indirectly before an audience, such as motion pictures, screenplays, musical works (including accompanying words), pantomimes, dramatic works (including accompanying music), choreographic works, and any other audiovisual works.

VA – Created for registering published or unpublished works in the area of visual arts, this area includes two-dimensional and three-dimensional works of fine art, graphic or applied art, photographs, prints, art reproductions, maps, gloves, charts, technical drawings, diagrams, models, architectural designs, sculptures, and jewelry.

TX – While one might expect this form to be named "lw," as it is used for registering published or unpublished nondramatic literary works (except for periodicals or serial issues), the letters actually refer to the fact that the work is text. This area includes fiction, nonfiction, poetry, textbooks, reference works, directories, catalogs, advertising copy, compilation of information, and computer programs.

SR – This form is used for registering published or unpublished sound recordings, if the copyright claim is limited to the sound recording itself. It can also be used if the claimant is also seeking simultaneous registration for the underlying musical, dramatic or literary work within the recording. Sound recordings are the result of a fixation of a series or musical, spoken, or other sounds, except for the audio portions of a audiovisual work (motion picture soundtrack or audio cassette accompanying a filmstrip). These audio portions are considered part of the whole audiovisual work.

RE – This form is used to file renewals when necessary.

SE – Keeping with using the first two letters of a subject, the SE form is used for registering individual issues of a serial, periodicals, newspapers, annuals, journals, proceedings, or transactions of societies. If one wishes to register an individual contribution to a serial, the TX form is appropriate.

The names of several of the forms do not easily relate to their subject matter.

GR/CP – Used for group contributions to periodicals, such as a weekly magazine with articles by different authors, this document must be filed with forms TX, PA, or VA.

G/DN – This form is used for registering daily newspapers. The claim must include all issue dates within the calendar month of the same year.

A microfilm form for the issues must be submitted. Each issue should essentially be an all-new collective work. The works must be work for hire, the authors and claimants are the same organization or person, and the application must be filed within three months of the last publication date in the group. If these conditions are not met, the SE Form applies.

CA – This form is used for correcting errors that occur in the registrations of copyrights. The previous application must have been duly registered. The Copyright Office will not accept Forms CA that do not show a registration number that is incorrect or incomplete. The Form CA is not used to reflect transfer of rights.

Works created under the General Agreement on Tariffs and Trade are protected by using the following special forms:

GATT/GRP – This form applies to group contributions for registering works in which U.S. Copyright Act was restored under the General Agreement on Tariffs and Trade.

GATT – This form is used to register copyright claims in a work in which the U.S. Copyright was restored under the 1994 Uruguay Round Agreements Act (URAA).

In addition, certain documents do not fit into any of the above-listed categories but still transfer copyright. In this situation, a copyright owner will use a document cover sheet.

As the name implies, the **document cover sheet** is attached to the top of these unconventional documents and is used for recording any assignment, mortgage, bankruptcy, or transfer of rights. The Copyright Office needs two copies of the cover sheet. When filling out the form, a signature is always required in Space 9 of the cover sheet. A signature is also required in Space 10 of the cover sheet if a copyright owner is sending a copy of the document instead of the original document. All documents are returned once the Copyright Office records the transfer.

The Deposit

In addition to the $20 registration fee, a specimen of the work being submitted must accompany the form. This can include a manuscript, a copy of a film or video cassette, or a synopsis of the film, the software program, or sample swatches of fabric patterns.

The U.S. Copyright Office distinguishes between published and unpublished works in terms of the required deposit. A **published work** is a work that has been released to the public: movies that are in theaters or video stores, books for sale in book stores, or records sold in record stores. **Unpublished** refers to works in progress or works that have not been released to the public. Generally, two specimens or sample copies must be submitted for published works; one copy is required for unpublished works.

One exception is in the visual arts category. Works such as paintings and sculptures are not considered as published if there is only one copy available. For example, a statue erected in a public square is not considered published, but reproductions of that statue available in stores are considered published works.

Another exception is in the performing arts category. The Copyright Office does not require two copies of a motion picture, even though the film has been released in movie theaters.

Completing the Forms

All forms must have an original signature. The form must be presented as it is printed by the Copyright Office. Copyright registration forms are two-sided and must be submitted in this same format. Photocopying a form is acceptable so long as it is two-sided, front and back. Two separate pieces of paper, even though they constitute a copy of the form, will be rejected.

Other Requirements

The Copyright Office usually requires a cover letter for all materials submitted for registration. The letter can be short and usually involves a simple inventory of the items being submitted (forms, fees, specimens).

The Copyright Specimen

Different specimens are required for different types of works. Knowing the specific requirements ahead of time can save time and trouble. Computer software is especially difficult. Usually the entire program is not required. Limited pages detailing the source codes or object codes can be submitted. The inclusion of secret information or previously copyrighted data in the deposit of these codes should be noted in a cover letter.

Another difficult area for filing a specimen is in the visual arts category. For three-dimensional objects like statues and jewelry, photographs can be submitted. For board games, a two-dimensional depiction (photograph or photocopy) can be submitted. For globes and relief or three-dimensional maps, one copy of the original work of published items must be submitted. For unpublished works, photocopies or pictures are acceptable.

Information on these and any other filing issues are available in a series of circulars published by the Copyright Office. There are approximately 50 pamphlets in the circular series. They can be obtained at a U.S. Government Printing Office book store or by calling the Copyright Office. Other sources for obtaining these circulars are libraries or research companies that specialize in this type of work.

What Does One Get in Return?

A certificate of registration is issued. The Copyright Office keeps the original specimen that was submitted with the original filing.

OTHER FILINGS

Recordations

As with assignments of patents and trademarks, assignments of copyrights are routinely filed. The term "assignment" refers to, transfers, security agreements, loans, mortgages, name changes or any transaction on a work.

The form for submitting assignments is called the "Document Cover Sheet." Information on this form includes assignor, assignee, nature of conveyance, title of the work involved, date of execution, fees, registration numbers, authors (if available), and corresponding address. The fee for filing assignments is $20, the same as filing for registration, plus an additional $10 for each group of 10 (or fewer) titles listed on the agreement.

Processing assignment recordations takes two to four months. As with registrations, expedited services for recordations are available for a fee of $350 for the first title plus the additional $10 per 10 or fewer titles listed on the agreement. Expedited turnaround time is one to two weeks.

TERMS OF PROTECTION

Initial Terms

For works created after January 1, 1978, the term of a copyright is the life of the author plus 50 years. Works created between January 1, 1964, and December 31, 1977, are protected for 28 years. These works are automatically renewed for 47 years after the end of the initial registration period. Works created before January 1, 1964, are also protected for an initial 28-year term, but these works must be renewed during the 28th year for the next 75 years. Works in the public domain prior to January 1, 1978, cannot be protected any further.

Renewals

A renewal must be filed by the end of the calendar year for the year in which it is due. A copyright does not have to be renewed specifically by the date on which it was originally registered.

Processing Time for an Application

The effective date of a copyright registration coincides with the filing date. It takes approximately six months to process a registration application. The Copyright Office receives thousands of filings every day. Turnaround time is dictated by the volume of registrations, renewals, and assignments to be processed. Expedited service takes approximately five to seven business days and is available for a fee of $350.

CHAPTER QUESTIONS

The Copyright Application

1.   A person approaches you wanting to file copyright applications for an unpublished manuscript of a novel and a necklace she has designed. What forms would be required?

2.   How long would a copyright last if it had been registered in 1935 by an author now deceased? Would there be any difference if the author were still living?

Chapter Nine

INTERNATIONAL COPYRIGHT PROTECTION

INTERNATIONAL COPYRIGHT LAW

In contrast to patent and trademark law, international copyright law affords protection to registered works in certain countries without a national filing of the copyright in each country. In fact, in many foreign countries, the copyright laws do not even provide for the registration of copyrights. With the exception of collective registers such as Benelux, AIPO or ARIPO,[1] patents and trademarks must be registered in each country in order to receive the full measure of protection and enforcement.

However, under two primary copyright treaties, a country will afford protection to a copyright that is not registered with its own government. In foreign countries, the protection of copyrighted works of United States authors and others is governed by the copyright laws of a country as well as by bilateral[2] and multilateral[3] international treaties.

Internationally, copyrights are governed by two primary conventions: the Bern Convention and the Universal Copyright Convention (UCC). Nearly every country in the world belongs to one of the two conventions; most belong to both.

THE BERN CONVENTION

The full name of the Bern Convention is the International Convention for the Protection of Literary and Artistic Works. It has become known as the Bern Convention because it was established in Bern,

---

[1] See Chapters Three and Six

[2] Between two countries

[3] Among three or more countries

Switzerland, in 1886. The basic purpose of the treaty is "for the protection of the rights of authors."[4]

The original Bern Convention of 1886 has gone through a number of revisions since its foundation. The first amendment and revision of the original Bern Convention took place in 1896 in Paris. Further revisions occurred in Berlin in 1908, in Bern in 1914, in Rome in 1928, in Brussels in 1948, in Stockholm in 1967, and in Paris in 1971. The 1971 revision is the most recent version in force.

The United States recently joined the Bern Convention. On October 31, 1988, President Reagan signed a bill amending the U.S. Copyright Act to make it compatible with Bern, and the U.S. took the formal steps necessary to become a member of Bern. The effective date of both the Act and the United States' membership in the Bern Convention is March 1, 1989. The Bern Convention is administered by the Word Intellectual Property Organization (WIPO) in Geneva, Switzerland.

The Bern Convention provides for four main areas of protection of copyright throughout the member countries.

First and most important, the Bern Convention provides for the national treatment[5] of copyrighted works; that is, an author's rights are respected in another country as though the author were a citizen of that country. For example, works of U.S. authors are protected in Austria by Austrian copyright law. Austrian works are, in turn, protected in the United States, since both countries are signatories to Bern.

Second, Bern provides for the preclusion of formalities.[6] Simply stated, this provision states that copyright protection cannot be dependent on formalities such as registration or copyright notice. An author does not need to provide written notice of his or her claim of copyright on a work to receive protection.

---

[4] Bern Convention, Article 1
[5] Article 5(1)
[6] Article 5(2)

Third, the Convention provides for a minimum term of protection.[7] Under Bern, the minimum duration for copyright protection is the life of the author plus 50 years. The member nations may provide longer durations if they so choose.

Finally, the Bern Convention provides for minimum exclusive rights.[8] A member nation must provide for protection of the following six rights:

The author of a copyright work shall have protection against

1. unauthorized translation
2. unauthorized reproduction
3. unauthorized public performance
4. unauthorized adaptation
5. paternity
6. integrity.

Paternity refers to the right always to claim to be the author of a work even if the ownership of the copyright is assigned. Integrity refers to the right to keep the work in a unified piece. In the United States, the rights of paternity and integrity only last for the life of the author.

UNIVERSAL COPYRIGHT CONVENTION

The United States has been a member of the Universal Copyright Convention (UCC) since 1954. Not as many countries belong to this convention as to the Bern Convention.[9]

The Universal Copyright Convention was originally written in 1952 in Geneva. It became effective in 1955. Like the Bern Convention, the UCC text has been revised. The most recent revision was executed in Paris in 1971. The United States is party to both the 1952 Geneva text

---

[7] Article 7(1)

[8] Article 8(1) in general, reproduction in Article 9(1), public performance in Article 11(1), adaptation in Article 12, and paternity and integrity in Article 6bis(1).

[9] Please refer to Table 2

and the 1971 Paris text. The UCC is administered by UNESCO, a United Nations agency.

Like Bern, the UCC requires national treatment for authors, but the UCC differs from Bern in four significant areas.

First, the UCC permits (but does not require) member states to require formalities such as copyright notice and registration.

Second, copyright duration must be until at least 25 years after the author's death or after the first publication, depending on whether a nation calculates duration based on the author's life or on publication.

Third, the UCC's provisions on minimum rights do not include paternity, integrity, and the right to perform or broadcast the work publicly.

Fourth, the UCC recognizes the Bern Convention. When a country is a member of both conventions, the Bern Convention will control, and the terms of the UCC will not apply.[10]

The United States was the primary influence behind the creation of the UCC, as U.S. copyright law at the time did not permit adherence to Bern. Since the United States joined Bern in 1988, the significance of the UCC has been declining.

COPYRIGHT NOTICE

In earlier versions of U.S. copyright law, the placement of the copyright notice on the work being claimed was required to receive protection under U.S. or international law. An author needed to put the world on notice by placing a copyright notice to the work.

While marking is no longer required, it is still customary and beneficial to place a notice on copyrighted works. The following is an example of a generally accepted format both in the United States and internationally:

---

[10] UCC Article XVII

"Copyright, 1997, The Smith Company, All Rights Reserved."

This notice contains four specific elements:

1. The term "Copyright" or the copyright symbol ("©")
2. The name of the owner of the copyright
3. The year of the copyright; which may include multiple years if the material was created and updated over a period of time
4. The phrase "All Rights Reserved."

As noted above, the copyright notice must also include the name of the owner of the copyright. This may either be an individual or group of individuals or may be a company if as in the given example, the work was made for hire. In works made for hire, the company is considered to be the author and owner of the work.

In order for American authors to preserve the copyright in their works in Bolivia, the Dominican Republic, Honduras and Uruguay, the provisions of the Buenos Aires Convention must be followed. Specifically, the phrase "All Rights Reserved," or a similar phrase must be placed on the mark.

MORAL RIGHTS

Article 6bis(1) of the Bern Convention specifically recognizes the moral rights of an author:

> Independently of the author's economic rights, and even after the transfer of the said rights, the author shall have the right to claim authorship of the work and to object to any distortion, mutilation or other modification of, or other derogatory action in relation to, the said work, which would be prejudicial to his honor or reputation.

Moral rights may be defined as the noneconomic rights which an artist acquires by creating a work of art. "Moral" rights are rights that either affect or have the potential to affect the artist's personality and reputation. These rights still exist for the author or artist even after the title of the copyright is transferred to another owner.

For example, a painter may sell a portrait of a woman to a private collector. In turn, this private collector may license the portrait to be used in part on a label for a cigarette package. Due to the moral rights as the creator of the original work, the original artist would have a right to prevent such a use. This type of right is different from the economic right assigned to the private collector.

The Bern Convention refers to the moral rights of "paternity" and "integrity."[11] The artist can claim the right to disclaim authorship of works the artist did not create, and the right to prevent public display of works by the artist that have been mutilated, distorted or altered. This right does not extend to alterations to the work that result from art conservation or the usual effects of time.

United States copyright law has traditionally only recognized and protected an artist's economic rights, such as the rights to copy, sell, or publicly display the artist's works. Before the passage of the current Act, artists' moral rights were protected primarily by enactments in a handful of states.

VISUAL ARTISTS RIGHTS ACT OF 1990

As mentioned above, the United States joined the Bern Convention in 1988. This meant that the United States needed to bring several aspects of its copyright law into compliance with Bern. Most changes involved the addition of "moral rights" to copyright law. The addition of moral rights brings the United States into compliance with the international considerations raised by the Bern Convention.

The 101st Congress enacted an amendment to the copyright law to create, for the first time, a federal statutory recognition of artists' moral rights in works of visual art.[12]

---

[11] See above.

[12] The Visual Artists Rights Act of 1990, Pub. L. No. 101-650, 601-610, 104 Stat. 5089, 5128 (1990) (codified at 17 U.S.C.S. § 106A (1988))

However, the Act covers only a single copy or limited edition of a work that was "produced for exhibition purposes only."[13] Therefore, the Act applies to "works of visual art" that are defined as works of fine art in limited editions of 200 or fewer and consecutively numbered, or one-of-a-kind pieces.

"Fine art" includes paintings, sculpture, prints, and photographs, but not motion pictures or "works made for hire." In contrast, the Act does not protect "colorized" motion pictures, among other things.

The Act brings U.S. copyright law into compliance with international law by granting visual artists the right of paternity, the right to disclaim paternity of the works that have undergone mutilation, distortion, or alteration, the right to prevent the attribution of the artist's name to works not created by the artist, and the right to bring a civil action, in the form of an infringement action or civil claim under the Copyright Act, for willful or negligent modification of the artist's works.

The rights conferred by the Act last for the life of the artist. Unlike economic copyright interests, which are transferable rights of property, the artist's rights under the Act cannot be transferred. These rights remain personal to the artist.

However, moral rights can be waived by the artist in a written document. To return to our example, the artist could consent in writing to the use of a portrait on a cigarette label. It should be noted that in the United States granting of the moral rights of paternity and integrity is much more limited than in most of the Bern Convention countries.

A PARALEGAL'S ROLE IN INTERNATIONAL COPYRIGHT PROTECTION

Research Country Law and Requirements

As with trademarks, the paralegal becomes a valuable resource in the enforcement of foreign copyright claims. Appendix Table 2 shows which countries adhere to the Bern Convention or UCC or both. Care

---

[13] 17 U.S.C. § 101

should be taken to research each country's laws individually. Generalizations, such as the ones in this book, do not allow the paralegal to understand the specific considerations for each country. This understanding comes through experience and research in available reference materials.

Liaison Between International Agent and Attorney

The paralegal can also take the initiative to ensure that all the information is communicated effectively between the foreign associate and the attorney. When a letter is received from a foreign associate, the paralegal should look for deadlines in the letter and retrieve any relevant country information for the attorney's review.

Liaison Between Client and Attorney

The paralegal can follow up on requests for information about a copyright held by a specific author. This follow-up can minimize or eliminate any misunderstandings or miscommunications between the attorney and the client.

CHAPTER QUESTIONS

International Copyright Protection

1.   What is the Bern Convention in the context of copyright protection?

2.   Is the phrase "All Rights Reserved" always required in a copyright notice? If not, is it ever required?

3.   An artist who is involved in animal rights sells his sculpture of a mother bear and cubs to a collector to raise money for his cause. He later finds out that the collector then sold the sculpture to a fur shop to attract business. Does the artist have any basis to object to the placement of the statue?

4.   What are the standards for copyright infringement?

EXERCISES

A.   Compose memos recommending a course of action for you and your attorney concerning the following fact patterns. Be certain to address questions about forms and procedures needed, as well as the research tools (refer to Tables 1 and 2) needed to accomplish each project.

   1.   A research assistant has developed a certain format for listing the telephone numbers of company employees. She shows you several company listings all in the same format and wants to copyright the lists.

   2.   A jewelry designer has been hired by a watch company to design a new line of men's and women's wrist watches. The designer has been asked to have you and your attorney register the copyright in the watches. She wants to own the copyrights because she is the designer. To prove her point she shows you a section in her work-for-hire contact that names her as the only designer of the line.

   3.   A manufacturer of playing cards from Denmark wants to start selling the cards in the United States. The cards have been registered with the Danish Copyright Office. The manufacturer is worried that he will have to take the time to register the cards in the United States.

B.   Referring to the forms described in Chapter Eight, list the type of United States Copyright application that would be needed for each of the following situations:

   1.   a new recording by a local band
   2.   a renewal of a previously registered copyright
   3.   a computer software program
   4.   a novel based on the writings of Shakespeare.
   5.   a collection of poems by unknown authors
   6.   a new training video incorporating elements (obtained with permission of the author) from a previously produced video.

Chapter Ten

OVERVIEW OF OTHER INTELLECTUAL PROPERTY AREAS

TRADE SECRETS

The law of trade secrets dates back to Roman law, which punished a person who induced another person to divulge secrets relating to the master's commercial affairs. The modern law of trade secrets evolved in England during the Industrial Revolution. The first reported trade secrets case in the United States dates back to 1837.[1]

Information, particularly competitive information, that is held secret by businesses is protected by trade secret law. This area of law protects such business information against unauthorized use or disclosure by anyone who acquired the information through improper methods or as a result of a confidential relationship with the trade secret holder.

Trade secrets remain out of the public domain, and their economic benefit is only exploited by the holder of the secret. This is in stark contrast to the subject inventions of patents, which pass into the public domain after the expiration of the patent. A patent, then, grants the owner a monopoly to exploit an invention for a limited time. As long as it remains a secret, a trade secret may be kept away from the public indefinitely.

For example, no one outside of the Coca-Cola Company knows the original formula for Coke. The formula has never been patented and remains a trade secret. Despite some questionable marketing in the mid-1980s, the formula for Coke remains a valuable and exploitable asset for the company. Its value to the company will only be lost if the secret is discovered and disseminated to the public.

---

[1] *Vickery v. Welch*, 36 Mass. 523 (1837)

It is often difficult to define a "secret," because the questions of free
competition and employee mobility are increasingly complex. United
States courts have based their trade secret decisions on two principles.

➢   The secret business information must be a valuable property to
       the business. That is, taking a secret of no value causes no
       harm to the company.

➢   The person(s) who are accused of disclosing the trade secret
       must have had a duty to respect the confidentiality of the
       information.

Although the states have enacted trademark or similar statutes, patent,
trademark, and copyright laws are dominated and governed by federal
statutes. By contrast, trade secret law remains largely a matter of
individual state law.

Each state is free to enact its own trade secret laws as long as the laws
do not conflict with federal intellectual property laws. The states' trade
secret laws are substantially similar, since they follow two major
sources in the 20th century:

        1.   The 1939 Restatement of Torts
        2.   The 1979 Uniform Trade Secrets Act.

Information Classified as a Trade Secret

A trade secret is information that must be secret and has commercial
value to the holder of the secret. Essentially, a trade secret may be
anything to which a court can be persuaded to give protection.

Paragraph 757 of 4 *Restatement of Torts* (1938) states that:

One who discloses or uses another's trade secret, without a
privilege to do so, is liable to the other if
        (a)   he discovered the secret by improper means, or
        (b)   his disclosure or use constitutes a breach of confidence
                 reposed in him by the other in disclosing the secret to
                 him, or

(c)   he learned the secret from a third person with notice of the facts that it was a secret and that the third person's disclosure of it was otherwise a breach of his duty to the other, or

(d)   he learned the secret with notice of the facts that it was a secret and that its disclosure was made to him by mistake.

Early in this century the courts have given a concise definition for this type of intellectual property:

> The term "trade secret" as it is usually understood means a secret formula or process, not patented, known only to certain individuals who use it in compounding or manufacturing some article of trade having a commercial value. It is rarely, if ever, used to denote the mere privacy with which an ordinary commercial business is carried on.[2]

When a court is persuaded that some information, such as a secret formula or process, is a genuine trade secret, then it will usually protect the trade secret against unauthorized disclosures to others or, if the trade secret has already been so disclosed, grant the owner of the lost secret monetary compensation for the unauthorized disclosure.

Essentially, any tangible piece of information can be a trade secret. As long as the information in question may be defined, it could qualify as a trade secret. The *Restatement of Torts* uses the phrase "a process or device"[3] to describe a trade secret. Thus, it is generally accepted that the subject of a trade secret claim must be more than an idea, theory, possibility, or anything ephemeral.

Trade secrets may also include nontechnical information such as sales data[4], price codes, marketing studies or marketing plans.[5] The

---

[2] *In re Bolster,* 110 P. 547, 548 (Wash. 1910)

[3] *Restatement of Torts* § 757

[4] *American Standard Inc v. Pfizer, Inc,* 828 F.2d 734 (Fed. Cir. 1987)

[5] *Clark v. Bunker*, 453 F.2d 1006 (9th Cir. 1972)

information must have competitive value for the holder of the secret and will cause competitive harm if the secret is disclosed to others.

The concept of harmful, or negative, information was considered by the Uniform Trade Secrets Act, which stated in a comment to Section 1 that a trade secret may be:

> Information that has commercial value from a negative viewpoint.. [For example]... the results of lengthy and expensive research which proves that a certain process will not work could be of great value to a competitor.

Secrecy of Idea

Neither the *Restatement of Torts* nor the Uniform Act of Trade Secrets Act offer an exact definition of "secrecy," but courts have discussed the concept at length. Trade secrets have become dependent on the concept of relative secrecy that determines how secrecy is maintained.

The Uniform Act notes that

> [R]easonable efforts to maintain secrecy have been held to include advising employees of the existence of a trade secret, limiting access to a trade secret on a "need to know basis," and controlling plant access. On the other hand, public disclosure of information through display, trade journal publications, advertising or carelessness can preclude protection.[6]

The growth of the scope and use of the Internet has added greatly to the issue of "reasonable efforts" to maintain secrecy. Information may be easily disseminated. For example, confidential papers about the research conducted on the failed Superconducting Supercollider in Texas were made available by research scientists on the project to the users of the Internet.

---

[6] Comment to § 1

Competitive Advantage of Idea

A trade secret must have value.[7] The secret must offer the owner some type of competitive advantage in the marketplace. The Uniform Act clearly states that a trade secret is an idea or concept from which its owner "derives independent economic value, actual or potential, from not being generally known to, and not being readily ascertainable by proper means by, other persons who can obtain economic value from its disclosure or use....[8]"

Interestingly, the Uniform Act's requirement for commercial value has excluded "spiritual" value from trade secret protection. The Church of Scientology tried to assert trade secret protection against an individual who posted secret, sacred teachings on the Internet. However, since the Church of Scientology asserted that these teachings only had spiritual value and not commercial value, it was denied trade secret protection.[9]

RIGHT OF PUBLICITY AND RIGHTS OF PRIVACY

Much like trade secret law, the right of publicity is a state-governed intellectual property law. In the simplest terms, the right to publicity is the right of every human being to control the commercial use of his or her identity and likeness. This right is not limited to people who are considered "celebrities" but is available to any individual, within the limits of the individual state's laws.

If a person can establish an aspect of his or her identity as a trademark, protection may be also be found in federal law. The federal Lanham Act[10] can offer protection where a person's identity is used to falsely advertise a product or designate its origin.

---

[7] *Restatement of Torts* § 757, comment b

[8] Uniform Trade Secrets Act §1(4)(i)

[9] *Religious Technology Center v. Wollersheim,* 796 F.2d 1091 (9th Cir. 1986), *cert denied* 479 U.S. 1103 (1987)

[10] See § 1125 of the Lanham Act.

The right to publicity actually means a right to maintain the privacy of one's identity and likeness. Privacy laws take on wide ranges of concepts and forums and have become a warehouse for many constitutional questions. For example, the well-known and controversial decision of *Roe v. Wade*[11] was a decision based on a woman's right to privacy. The *Roe* decision held that the "right of privacy," as expressed in the Ninth and Fourteenth amendments to the Constitution, was "broad enough to encompass a woman's decision whether or not to terminate her pregnancy."[12]

The right to publicity has grown out of a hybrid of several areas of the law. Its roots are found in the right to privacy and have been tempered by the laws of defamation, copyright, misappropriation, trademark, and false advertising. Most often, the right to privacy is employed when there are commercial considerations involved.

Public Figures

The right to publicity may be triggered when someone's image or persona is taken by a third party to promote the products or services of another. Typically, the amount of the damage is predicated on the value of a person's image. A celebrity is usually damaged quickly and deeply because of the value of their public image.

The courts have held that the celebrity's persona must be easily identifiable in any right to publicity case. This clearly covers photographs and images, but other distinctive traits also fall under the protection of the right to publicity.

In 1988 singer Bette Midler sued the Ford Motor Company,[13] which had featured in its commercials a Midler tune performed by a sound-alike. While Ford had obtained the copyright owner's permission to use the song, it had no agreement with Midler herself. The court held that "a voice is as distinctive and personal as a face...To impersonate her voice is to pirate her identity."

---

[11] 410 U.S. 113 (1973)

[12] *id.* at 153

[13] *Midler v. Ford Motor Co.*, 849 F.2d 460 (9th Cir. 1988)

Taking the concept even further, a court[14] held that an ad depicting a
robot in a wig posed on the set of a futuristic game show suggestive of
the *Wheel of Fortune* game show violated hostess Vanna White's right
of publicity. Samsung had featured a robot in a sequined dress and a
blond wig standing next to a letter game board with the caption
"longest running game show 2012 A.D." Although there was no
similarity between Vanna White's face and that of the robot, the court
held that the dress, wig, and proximity to the game board was a
misappropriation of Vanna's persona.

While being a celebrity affords a person more recognizable publicity
rights, this same aspect can limit his or her privacy claims. Actress
Elizabeth Taylor filed a lawsuit[15] in mid-August 1994 in California
Superior Court in Los Angeles against NBC, a television production
company, and an author to prevent the network from using her name or
likeness or using another actress to play her in a miniseries about her
life. Taylor argued that the miniseries should be enjoined because it
infringed upon her "right of publicity."

The court rejected that argument, explaining that the right of publicity
cannot be used to prevent commentary on the lives of public people.
The court ruled that an injunction against NBC would constitute an
unconstitutional prior restraint against First Amendment-protected
expression. The court first noted that prior restraints are generally
considered unconstitutional restrictions on free speech and granted only
in exceptional cases. The court explained that reproductions of past
events and biographies fall within the scope of protected First
Amendment expression.

Private Individuals

Rights to privacy are not denied to those who are not classified as
"celebrities." As early as 1902, a young woman named Abigail
Robeson asserted her rights in her image[16] when the Rochester Folding

---

[14] *White v. Samsung Electronics America, Inc.,* 971 F.2d 1395 (9th Cir. 1992),
cert denied 113 S.Ct. 2443 (1993)

[15] *Taylor v. NBC*, No. BC 110922 (Cal. Super. Ct. Sept. 29, 1994)

[16] *Robeson v. Rochester Folding Box Co.,* 64 NE 442 (1902)

Box Company used a photograph of Ms. Robeson on its packaging for Franklin Mills Flour with the slogan "Flour of the Family."

Ms. Robeson complained that her image was displayed in various places including those of ill-repute, such as saloons, and that she had been humiliated. The New York court did not side with Ms. Robeson. The public outrage to the opinion caused the New York legislature to enact one of the first publicity statutes.

More recently, when an Ohio television station filmed a performer's entire 15-second human cannonball act for its evening newscast, the U.S. Supreme Court found that the film posed a substantial threat to the economic value of that performance. Therefore, use of the film was a misappropriation of the cannonball performer's professional property.[17]

In a 1993 case,[18] the U.S. Court of Appeals for the Sixth Circuit ordered a district court judge to vacate his order preventing distribution of a book with a jacket containing a photograph of a murder victim with red ink splattered on it to look like a blood stain.

The judge issued the order after the victim's sister filed suit claiming that the jacket violated the victim's "right of publicity." In their decision to vacate the judge's order, the court of appeals stated that "even minimal interference with First Amendment freedoms causes injury."

Right to publicity cases remain a confusing mixture of the different bodies of law. Each case is decided on its own merits in the different courts and provide different precedents, depending on which of the other laws, such as trademark or First Amendment, are present in the case.

---

[17] *Zachini v. Scripps-Howard Broadcasting Company*, 433 U.S. 562 (1997)
[18] *Hogg v. Harper Collins Publishers, Inc.*, No. Cir-93-142 (E.D. Ky. April 12, 1993)

CHAPTER QUESTIONS

Overview of Other Intellectual Property Areas

1.   An engineer designs a special type of blade for a blender that makes his company's blenders very successful. He is later hired by a competitor. Is the engineer prevented from designing another special type of blade for a blender?

2.   You are walking down the street and happen to be photographed next to a famous celebrity walking out of a hotel. Later the photograph is used in a magazine ad campaign for champagne. Do you and the celebrity have any recourse about this use of the photograph? Is there any difference in this situation between you and the celebrity?

Chapter Eleven

LEGALIZATION AND AUTHENTICATION OF DOCUMENTS

By Tim Ralston
Thomson & Thomson
Washington Services

DEFINITION OF LEGALIZATION

Legalization is an administrative procedure to make a document legally acceptable for filing in a foreign jurisdiction. In international business and legal transactions, documents accompanying the transaction often must be legalized in order to complete the transaction. Making documents lawful, or legalizing them, involves a series of administrative steps in which representatives of various governments notarize and approve documents in preparation for filing them overseas.

Even with lightning-fast communications and commercial barriers coming down between countries, it is still necessary to get documents legalized in much the same way it has been done for years. For the paralegal, legalization can be a time-consuming and frustrating process. Embassy procedures change; fees change. Even when no problems are encountered, there is still a maze of rules and bureaucracies to maneuver. The purpose of this chapter is to explain the process and to provide some guidance on how to accomplish the task of preparing documents for travel to another country.

DETERMINING WHEN LEGALIZATION IS REQUIRED

Any document can be legalized. What to legalize and when to have documents legalized depends on the country involved, the particular needs of the foreign agent or government agency, and the nature of the transaction. Powers of attorney and authorizations of agent are used when contracting with a foreign agent. Foreign government agencies might require business activity affidavits, certificates of incorporation, or other related material.

Foreign courts often require documents from corresponding domestic litigation. Normal document filing activity, such as foreign trademark and patent applications, often require the related U.S. trademark or patent documents be legalized.

Key issues in determining how to legalize documents are knowing the requirements of the foreign associate or agency and knowing which U.S. agency provides the documents you require.

In general, legalization involves three types of documents:

1.   those that are privately drafted
2.   those that are issued by state regulatory agencies
3.   those that are issued by the federal government.

Different steps are involved in legalizing each of these three types of documents.

LEGALIZATION PROCESS

Privately Drafted Documents

For our purposes, **privately drafted** means any document *not* issued by a government agency. These include powers of attorney, authorizations of agent, affidavits, declarations, contracts, and assignments, to name a few. The first step is having the document notarized, which is standard for many legal documents. Usually, the notary acts as a witness to the signing of documents.

For legalization, the notary public seal makes the document ready for the next step, preparing the document for overseas filing. Most law firms, banks, real estate agencies, and businesses have a registered notary, and this notary is sometimes available to people walking in off the street. Fees and other regulations vary from state to state. Secretary of state offices are usually responsible for registering notaries, so questions about notary fees and procedures can be directed to those state offices.

The next step for the notarized document is obtaining the state's secretary of state certificate of the notary signature. This is relatively easy, since the secretary of state's office is responsible for registering notaries. The certificate that is issued merely attests to the fact that the person who witnessed and notarized the document is a registered notary in that state.

Fees and turnaround times vary, so it is best to call ahead to get exact information to speed up the process. When sending documents to a secretary of state, a letter should be attached briefly describing the documents and, most important, the country in which they are being filed. Where the document is going dictates the type of certificate to be attached.

Nothing will save more time than getting procedures right the first time. Giving the secretary of state as much information as possible will promote speedy completion. There is no rule about turnaround times. Larger or more populous states may take longer; many offer expedited services for an additional fee. In all cases, it is best to include a self-addressed envelope for return mailing.

Some states require that a county clerk or clerk of courts certify the notary signature. In this instance, the secretary of state will certify to the clerk's signature. New York is one such state. A document that has been notarized by a Manhattan notary must have the notary signature certified by the Manhattan county clerk before being sent to the secretary of state's office. The secretary of state will certify to the certificate of the Manhattan county clerk. All of this adds steps to the process; however, most states do not require this. A call to the secretary of state beforehand will clear up any such issues and will help in proceeding smoothly.

Authentication

The next step involves the United States Department of State. This is called **authentication** and involves the secretary of state for the United States attesting to the certificate issued by the secretary of state of the state in which the document originated and was notarized.

Authentication means that the United States secretary of state officially recognizes the authenticity of the signature of the state secretary of state. This is the last step before sending documents to foreign consulates. Countries that require legalization usually require documents be authenticated by the U.S. Department of State before the country will legalize the documents. Authentication is also required when certified documents from a federal agency are involved.

Authentication may be accomplished in two ways. Documents may either be hand-delivered for immediate processing by the State Department's Authentication Office, or they can be mailed. There are advantages to both methods, but timeliness and cost are the biggest factors.

Walk-in service involves hand-delivery of up to 15 documents per day. It usually takes about 30 minutes to complete the maximum number of documents and, when done, they are ready to be taken to the appropriate consulate for legalization. The Authentication Office is open to the public only four hours per day, and there is a limit of one visit per customer. When completed, documents can usually be delivered to a consulate on the same day.

Many people prefer hand-delivering their documents, either by an agent specializing in dealing with these matters or by a reliable courier. By using the walk-in service, any problems that arise can be handled quickly, thus avoiding any delays in getting documents to a consulate for legalization. Couriers and agents charge fees ranging from $10 to $150.

The mail-in service has no limits on the number of documents that can be sent, but it does take slightly longer to complete. With a self-addressed return envelope or overnight courier package, documents are completed and returned in five to ten business days. Sending documents directly to the Authentication Office eliminates the need for and the costs of using an agent or courier. However, problems with documents will not be resolved as easily, and valuable time might be lost if documents are returned for corrections.

Many foreign governments maintain satellite consulates and ask that documents originating from certain regions be legalized only by the local consulate for that region or group of states. Again, timeliness is the issue. Documents can be sent to the State Department for authentication and returned to be taken to the local consulate, or they can be hand-delivered to the office for more immediate processing.

The document is now ready to go to the embassy for legalization. It has been notarized by a notary public, certified by a state secretary of state, and authenticated by the U.S. Department of State.

Federal Government Documents

Documents produced by federal government agencies can also be legalized. Depending on the document required, agencies will certify as to the information contained in their documents. Certification usually requires a fee. Documents are attested to by a certifying office or agent within the agency. Certified documents from federal agencies are recognized by the U.S. State Department when they are to be authenticated.

For example, certified copies of U.S. trademark registrations and applications can be obtained from the U.S. Patent and Trademark Office. A copy of the requested document is produced, and a certified letter is attached attesting to the current status and ownership of the registration or application. Other documents that are routinely certified for legalization include copyright registrations, patents, and federal court documents, to name but a few.

Only the U.S. State Department can authenticate federal government documents. This includes regular authentication as part of a legalization or an apostille. An apostille is a simplified certification of a notarized document allowed by countries belonging to the Hague Convention.

EMBASSIES

Fees, turnaround times and other regulations are different for every country. A partial listing of embassies and their charges is included in Appendix Table 2. For additional information, two publications by the U.S. Department of State are available from the U.S. Government Printing Office. The Diplomatic List[1] includes embassies with addresses, phone and fax numbers, consulates, and the primary officers in Washington, DC. Foreign Consular Offices in the United States[2] lists consulates in cities across the United States. This publication is arranged alphabetically by country and also includes addresses, phone and fax numbers, and main consular officers at each location.

Many countries do not have consulates anywhere other than Washington, DC. Other countries have consulates in regions that serve a particular interest. For example, a Central American nation might have a consulate in Miami or Houston or Atlanta, but not in Chicago or Seattle, whereas an Asian country will have offices on the West Coast, but not in Atlanta or Miami.

Some countries require documents be legalized only by the consulate nearest the city where the documents originated. The Taiwanese consulate in Washington, DC, will legalize documents only from the region that includes Virginia, Maryland, Delaware and North Carolina. Outside of this area, the documents have to be sent to a different consulate for legalization.

As of the publication of this book, there are three countries with which the United States has no official diplomatic contact: Cuba, Iraq, and Libya. Documents going to Cuba can be legalized by using the Cuban Interest Section of the Swiss embassy in Washington, DC. Iran also operates in similar fashion within the Pakistani embassy.

---

1. Department of State Publication 7894
2. Department of State Publication 7846

THE HAGUE CONVENTION
OF OCTOBER 1961

The Hague Convention is an international treaty designed to streamline the process of filing documents overseas by eliminating many of the steps involved with legalization. Countries that have signed the agreement accept documents that have been affixed with an apostille. Apostilles are more easily obtained and require far fewer steps than having documents taken in and out of state agencies, the State Department and an embassy.

For documents of local origin, the secretary of state for that state can affix an apostille to a notarized document. For federal government documents, the U.S. Department of State attaches the apostille to the certified document from the issuing agency. Once affixed with apostille, the document is ready to be filed with the foreign agency or department.

Countries that are members of the Hague Convention include most of Europe and North America, Japan, Panama, Argentina, El Salvador and Mexico. Documents being filed in these countries can be done by obtaining an apostille from either the state secretary of state or the U.S. Department of State, for documents issued by federal government agencies. A complete list of countries is attached in appendix Table 5.

CHAPTER QUESTIONS

Legalization and Authentication of Documents

1.   Why would anyone want to "legalize" a document? When, if ever, would it be necessary?

2.   Can the U.S. Treasury Department issue a privately drafted document?

3.   How does the Hague Convention affect the legalization process for a document?

EXERCISES

Your client has just completed a foreign filing program for its
trademarks. Powers of attorney are now being requested by the
individual agents in the countries. For the following countries, please
indicate what level of legalization may be required and if there are any
special considerations:

1.	Singapore	11.	Denmark
2.	Australia	12.	Cuba
3.	Great Britain	13.	Latvia
4.	Thailand	14.	India
5.	France	15.	Iraq
6.	Mexico	16.	The Bahamas
7.	Brazil	17.	China (mainland)
8.	Japan	18.	Yugoslavia
9.	Jordan	19.	Canada
10.	Haiti	20.	Italy

Chapter Twelve

PATENT, TRADEMARK AND COPYRIGHT SEARCHING

THE REQUIREMENT TO SEARCH INTELLECTUAL PROPERTY

In general, no one is entitled to protection of any type of intellectual property if that property belongs to another party. For example, Section 1051(1)(A) of the Lanham Act clearly states that the owner of a trademark may submit a written application if, among other requirements, that applicant must make a verified statement

> ...[T]o the effect that the person making the verification believes himself or herself, or the firm, corporation, or association in whose behalf he or she makes the verification, to be entitled to use the mark in commerce, and that no other person, firm, corporation, or association, to the best of his or her knowledge and belief, has the right to use such mark in commerce either in the identical form of the mark or in such near resemblance to the mark as to be likely, when used on or in connection with the goods of such other person, to cause confusion, or to cause mistake, or to deceive.

Similarly, a patent cannot be granted unless it is shown that invention must be new and original (novel) in comparison to other similar ideas and inventions.

When the owner of a patent, trademark or copyright property approaches an attorney with a request to determine whether or not that property is protectable or even valid, the attorney must obtain a current and accurate search of the resources available to be able to provide a responsible opinion to the client.

In the past, all searches were conducted manually through independent search firms in Washington, DC. An attorney or interested party may also contract for a search by one of the many search firms such as Orbit, Thomson & Thomson or Corsearch.

In many firms and corporations, the paralegal has assumed the responsibility of conducting the searches. Although there is no guaranteed method of determining that every possible property has been searched, there are certain methods and precautions that can be taken to ensure that the search results are as comprehensive and up-to-date as possible.

DEFINING THE SCOPE OF THE SEARCH

Before the search process begins, the paralegal needs to define the scope of the search and plan the resources that will be reviewed during the search. Forethought about the search strategy is important, as many resources for searching charge per minute of connect time. The paralegal's time is a valued commodity and should not be wasted in repetitious or superfluous search efforts.

Although they contain similar elements, patent, trademark, and copyright searching should be defined with different considerations.

1.   A person planning a **patent search** should consider the following factors:

        a)   *Area of the invention* - The searcher must determine the field of the invention, whether it is chemical in nature, physical or computer-related. A good knowledge of the area will allow the searcher to identify resources for conducting a prior art search.

        b)   *Common terms in the industry* - What is uncommon in one area may be a term of art in another. Access to an industry glossary of terms will help the searcher understand key terms when formulating a search strategy, either for online searching or for the manual search of patent literature.

2.   To determine the scope of the **trademark search**, the mark
should be broken down into the following factors:

   a)   *Length and size of the mark* – The searcher must
determine the length of the mark and break the mark down into
different smaller elements that may function as a trademark on their
own apart from the mark as a whole. The longer the mark, the more
analysis of the element words and phrases will be required.

   b)   *Proposed use of the mark* – It is important to
determine what specific goods and/or services will be identified by the
mark being searched. As mentioned earlier, the same mark can be used
in different fields. Identifying the goods and services will help keep the
search focused for the attorney and for the client.

   c)   *Meaning of the mark* – Does the mark mean anything
to anyone in the field of search? For that matter, it is worthwhile to
determine if the mark has any common meaning in any field.
Remember, a generic mark cannot function as a trademark. An
effective search tool for trademarks is a comprehensive dictionary.
Marks appearing in a dictionary can be considered to be arbitrary and
are very likely generic.

Also, remember that acronyms can function as trademarks and can also
be generic. Your client may tell you that its use of the term "LEC"
may refer to a special type of hammer or weather stripping. However,
if your client is a telecommunications company and this mark refers to
its local telephone services, then the mark would not be registerable
because "LEC" in the telecommunication industry refers to "local
exchange carrier."

   d)   *Phonetics of the mark* – Try to determine any alternate
phonetics to the mark. Oftentimes, the vowels in a mark are
interchangeable with other words. "DUCK" and "DECK" are only one
vowel apart. Also, words often have many forms and with different
endings can functions as nouns, verbs, and adjectives. A "sleeper" is a
noun; however, "sleep" and "sleeping" are verbs, and "sleepy" is an
adjective. To add to the variations, Walt Disney made the verb form
famous as a noun when he gave it to one of the seven dwarfs in the
movie *Snow White*.

e)   ***Variations of the mark*** – There are often alternate spellings for the same mark. Some of these alternate spellings are used daily, such as "BEAR" and "BARE." Many of the spellings are invented by trademark owners and rely on identical sounding spellings, such as "CYBER" and "SYBER."

The best way to remember this principle is through a very short story: Once a very individualistic man brought a dog home from the pound. Since he did not want to be like everyone else, he did not want to give the canine an ordinary name. After much thought, he decided to name his new friend "Phydeaux" (phonetically, "Fido").

3.   To determine the scope of a **copyright search,** the searcher will need to determine the following:

a)   ***The medium used for the copyrighted material*** – The searcher will need to determine how the work is fixed (that is, made permanent). The person must determine if the work is printed, or painted, the subject of a performance, or any other method of fixing. This will help the searcher focus in the correct area of copyright registrations, for the medium is as important as the subject.

b)   ***The name of the work and the author*** – Both of theses names will give the searcher terms to use to narrow the scope of the search within a medium.

ACCESSING ONLINE DATABASES

Many intellectual property databases are now available online either through dial-up modems or the Internet. Depending on the database searched, a person can find fairly current records for U.S. federal, state, and several foreign patent and trademark offices. The records are usually updated monthly. It is important to check with each database service provider.

Generally, online databases can be accessed through what is known as a dial-up account; that is, a searcher uses a modem that dials a particular computer server directly. These databases require that an account be in place. The user will be given a password to verify the right to search the records in the database.

Online databases are searched through a set of defined query terms. Query terms refer to a method of organizing a search request. These terms vary from database to database. The most common method of organizing a search is called boolean search logic.

A boolean expression is a combination of comparison expressions or matching expressions, using the boolean operators "or," "and," and "not," along with parentheses to the control structure of the search. The relevance of the boolean expression is computed by combining the truth values of the component expressions. Any items that match the "relevance" of the search is retrieved by the database.

The boolean "and" expression allows you to narrow a search in order to retrieve items containing information on the topic you are researching. You can find information about crab apples by typing "(crab and apple)" in your query.

The boolean "or" expression allows you to broaden a search. Typically, you will use the boolean "or" search to find synonyms to do the broadest possible search of a database. The boolean "or" search usually retrieves large numbers of results. Therefore, you will often follow up by combining your boolean "or" search with a boolean "and" search.

The boolean "not" allows you to eliminate from your search items that include a specific keyword. The boolean "not" search is not frequently used, as it is very limiting. For example, a quick way to find any references to the play *Hamlet* that do not include the author is to enter the query "(*Hamlet* not Shakespeare)."

Using a combination of boolean or any search logic will help you refine the search to fit the criteria of the use of the mark. If you are inexperienced at searching, it is best to plan the search before accessing the database, as each database charges for connect as well as search time.

Specific examples of searching patent, trademark and copyright databases are shown through actual examples reprinted by permission of Knight-Ridder Corporation at Appendix Table 9.

THE MANUAL SEARCH

It is important to remember that, even at the close of the 20th century, not every bit of information is available by computer. The different areas of intellectual property still have requirements for manual searches.

Search for Early Patents, Published Papers and Articles

To explore an area of an invention fully, a searcher must often go beyond the printed patents. Ideas or concepts in a particular field are often only the subject of published papers and trade articles. These resources are still housed in technical libraries and depositories such as universities and even the patent offices.

Many inventors are surprised to have their applications invalidated by the finding of a thesis paper or research study from a major university. Published papers and articles are still best found manually by sending a searcher to the actual university, medical facility or government office.

Patent databases do not carry full records of existing patents that were granted prior to 1977. It is still necessary to travel to an actual Patent and Trademark Depository Library (PTDL) to obtain copies of these earlier patents. A list of the current PDTL libraries is found in Table 4.

The Manual Design Mark Search

Many trademark search requests involve designs either as part of the mark or as the entire mark. Designs have only recently been added to several of the available commercial databases. The search logic and coding (the method that identifies the various elements of a design) has not been standardized.

The worst danger in relying on electronic searching is that these databases are usually not complete. They have records that only date back to a certain year within the last 30 years. While this may sound comprehensive enough, if a person is searching for designs for ropes and cords featuring strongmen and lions (such as the previously mentioned SAMSON and design trademark registration mentioned on page 34), then the researcher may be disappointed.

A database would likely not carry records back to the last century (see page 35 for a registration dating back to 1884.) The most reliable method of design searching is to contract with a service that will conduct a manual search at the records of the Trademark Office. These records are kept in individual drawers known as "shoes" and are still arranged according to the national classification system used in the United States prior to the passage of the Lanham Act in 1947.

The Manual Copyright Registration Search

Copyright records are the most voluminous and most elusive to find online. The records are maintained by the Library of Congress, and the actual deposits are often warehoused in its dark interior chambers.

As of this writing, the most accurate method of searching for copyrights and title properties is through a manual search at the Library of Congress. The records and cross-references can be followed much more accurately by an individual pulling the references than by a searcher relying on references in a database.

SEARCH FOR COMMON LAW
USES OF TRADEMARKS

All trademark uses and users are not found either in the federal or state records. Many trademark owners do not register their marks for a number of reasons. Therefore, it is important to check available resources.

Some of the most useful resources are the computerized records of the corporate records of the various secretaries of states. These will reveal any party that uses the mark as part of its company's name.

Also, numerous magazines, newspapers, and trade journals are available online. A search of the news sources allows you to find many uses of marks that are announced but are not necessarily the subject of an application. Finally, many different companies, such as Dun & Bradstreet and American Business Information, offer compilations of company names. These resources can identify companies that operate under unregistered assumed names or partnerships that are not registered with any state body.

Any significant references that are found in the common law searches will eventually need to be verified. The only sure method of verification is through direct contact, such as a telephone call. These telephone investigations can be difficult, as many people become suspicious of questions about the use of their names and marks.

While many different approaches are used in telephone investigations, it is important to keep in mind that information found through deception during the investigation will open the searcher to charges of fraud and may invalidate any eventual trademark registration.

WORLD WIDE WEB

It is now hard to imagine life without the World Wide Web, but it has not always existed. Its nature is a bit of a mystery to the end-user. Simply put, the Internet, or World Wide Web, is a network of networks. It is a network that spans much of the earth.

All of these networks have in common their use of the Internet protocols, or the way the computers "talk" to one another. Computers, acting as switches, serve as gateways connecting the various networks together.

The computers can also translate messages to and from other computers that use different communications protocols. The gateways use the Internet addressing scheme to move packets of information that can include text, audio, and even video, back and forth. Packets are passed from one computer (or node) to another until the final destination is reached.

If a particular pathway is unavailable, the packet is rerouted automatically by the computer switches. Upon arriving at their final destination, the packets are automatically reassembled. Typically, only a few seconds will pass from the time the request is initiated until it completed.

Internet Basics

There are now approximately 40 million users of the World Wide Web, with approximately 150,000 servers and over 100 million web pages. It has been estimated that the web grew sixfold in 1996 and that the size of the Web is doubling every 57 days.

Domain Names

A domain name consists of the following two parts: the name of the company or institution followed by a generic abbreviation identifying the type of organization (or country, outside the United States): for example, "microsoft.com."

A.   The Top-Level Name. The Internet users are classified in different categories, depending upon the nature of the organization. A generic abbreviation is assigned to the domain name that appears to the right of the period. The top-level names currently consist of the following seven categories:

1.   *.edu* for educational organizations
2.   *.com* for commercial entities
3.   *.net* for computers of network providers such as InterNIC
4.   *.int* for international databases and organizations established by international treaties
5.   *.org* for other organizations
6.   *.gov* for federal government offices and agencies
7.   *.mil* for the United States military.

It was announced on February 5, 1997, that seven new generic top-level names would be created in addition to the existing

ones. As of November 1997 the names have not been
implemented. However, the new names will be:

8.   *.firm* for businesses or firms
9.   *.store* for businesses offering goods to purchase
10.   *.web* for entities emphasizing activities related to the
        World Wide Web
11.   *.arts* for entities emphasizing cultural and entertainment
        activities
12.   *.rec* for entities emphasizing cultural and entertainment
        activities
13.   *.info* for entities providing information services
14.   *.nom* for those wishing individual or personal
        nomenclature.

Outside of the United States, the generic abbreviation is not
used. Instead, country abbreviations are used, such as ".uk" for
the United Kingdom or ".mx" for Mexico, along with
additional identifiers that tend to vary from country to country
such as ".co" for a commercial site. Thus, the Smith Company
in Mexico might have the domain name of "smith.co.mx."

B.   The Second-Level Name. The second part of the domain name
        appears to the left of the period and acts as the source
        identifier. This is the "second-level" domain name. In the
        example "gte.com," the second-level name is "gte." This name
        identifies the host computer.

        The second-level domain name is acquired only through
        registering it with the Internet Network Information Center,
        known as "InterNIC." This is where all of the trademark
        disputes have arisen.

C.   The Lower-Level Name. The domain name may be further
        distinguished through the use of lower-level domain names to
        the left of the second-level domain name. For example, the
        third-level name in the address "telops.gte.com" is "telops."

        Additional lower-level names may be added. None of the
        lower-level names require registration with InterNIC.

Using the Internet Search Engines

New ways to find information have grown in recent years along with the growth of the Internet itself. Surfing was the typical approach for finding information on the Web. **Surfing** refers to unstructured searching that basically blindly follows links to links in a haphazard manner. While surfing is fun, it is without structure and does not allow search strategy.

A number of new tools, known as search engines, have been developed that enable a searcher to find information published on the Internet in a structured manner.

Search engines feature indexes that are automatically compiled by computer programs, such as robots and tools that are known as "spiders," that go out over the Internet to discover and collect Internet resources. Searchers can connect to a search engine site and enter keywords to query the index. Web pages and other Internet resources that satisfy the query are identified and listed.

Search engines vary according to the size of the index, the frequency of updating the index, the search options, the speed of returning a result set, the result set presentation, the relevancy of the items included in a result set, and the overall ease of use.

Well-known search engines include Webcrawler, Lycos, and InfoSeek, Excite, Alta-Vista, Yahoo and MetaCrawler. All these engines use keywords to build subject-specific indexes. MetaCrawler actually threads several other search engines together to offer a type of "all-in-one" search.

INTELLECTUAL PROPERTY SEARCHES ON THE INTERNET

The resources on the Internet have become invaluable to the searcher in determining both use of references found in the traditional databases and any common law references that are not found in any prior search.

In the days before the Internet, it was very difficult to find vague uses of a trademark or references to inventions. Now there is an abundance of sites by people and organizations volunteering information. The best attitude to use when searching the Internet is to assume that there is a reference to the mark you are researching. The Internet is best explored through the use of search engines.

Also, domain names can function as trademarks as they identify the locations of goods and service providers on the World Wide Web. Not surprisingly, many lawsuits arose as famous marks were "pirated." One of the most famous, *MTV Networks v. Adam Curry,* 867 F.Supp. 202 (S.D.N.Y. 1994), involved a former MTV "video jockey" (VJ), who, while employed at MTV, had registered "mtv.com" under his own name with the company's approval. When he left MTV, he refused to give up the domain. Eventually, MTV and Curry settled with MTV's gaining control of the name.

It has become very important to research the use of a mark as a domain name. The two best methods of searching domain names are either through the InterNIC naming authority itself at its "whois" site, located at "http://rs.internic.net/cgi-bin/whois," or searching Thomson & Thomson's domain name database site located at "http://www.thomson-thomson.com."

The best approach a searcher can take in approaching the Internet is to believe that the information is actually there and keep trying. More often than not, this assumption will be correct. As there are no longer any per-minute charges, a searcher can keep trying and perfecting search strategy with little loss but his or her own time.

CHAPTER QUESTIONS

Patent, Trademark and Copyright Searching

1.   Why would you want to search for information pertaining to a patent, trademark or copyright property?

2.   A client has designed a new formula for correction fluid used in typing. It has designed a new bottle and wants to call the product

"It's Better than White." How would you define the scope of the searches required?

3.   Why is the Internet becoming so important to intellectual property searching?

GLOSSARY

abandonment

the failure to take all the steps to complete the application process

abstract

a concise paragraph found on the front page of an issued patent certificate that briefly describes the workings and features of the invention

allowance

an acknowledgment by the governmental body that an application is eligible for registration; an eligible application is considered to be "allowed" for registration

amendment

an answer to an office action issued by a governmental body, usually modifying, correcting, or deleting elements of an original application

apostille

a simplified certification of notarized documents allowed by countries that belong to the Hague Convention. With an apostille the document is entitled to recognition in the country of intended use and no additional legalization is required

application

a request to a governmental body of a country to formally recognize an applicant's rights in an invention, trademark or copyright

artistic work

a visual representation such as a painting, drawing, map, photograph, sculpture, engraving or architectural plan

assignment

the transfer of intellectual property rights from the owner to another party

author

the creator of an artistic, literary, musical or dramatic work

Bern Convention

a copyright treaty established in Bern, Switzerland in 1886. The basic purpose of the treaty is for the protection of the rights of authors

Boolean Search Logic

a set of defined query terms based on comparative logic

certificate of registration

official confirmation of registration received from a governmental body

certification mark

a trademark that refers to a standard of quality for a product

claim

a section of a patent wherein the invention is specifically defined a grammatically correct numbered sentence. There may be more than one claim and the claims may be independent

collective mark

a trademark that signifies affiliation with an organization that has set certain standards for membership

compulsory license	a grant to use some form of intellectual property through a means set up by the government for a public interest
copyright	protection for the particular expression of an idea which is created and fixed in a tangible form, such as writing or an audiovisual work
disclaimer	a statement that a certain word or portion of a trademark or an element of an invention is not protected
European Patent Convention (EPC)	a treaty that provides a single procedure for granting one "European patent" to an invention which will be valid, upon payment of an appropriate fee, in all EPC member countries
examination	the procedures undertaken by a governmental body to ensure that the subject of an application should be granted registration
fair use	a limited use of a copyrighted work allowed without the copyright owner's permission
fees	specific sums required for governmental action on intellectual property examination, registration and maintenance

filing date
the date a completed application is officially received by the governmental body

first to file
a patent and/or trademark system in which the first inventor or trademark owner to file an application for a specific invention or mark is entitled registration

front page
a term used to describe the first page of an issued patent certificate

General Agreement on Tariffs and Trade (GATT)
an international agreement whose provisions affect international patent and trademark prosecution, protection and maintenance

genericide
the misuse of a trademark by the public that allows it to become a generic term in the field

Hague Convention (Abolishing the Requirement of Legalization for Foreign Public Documents)
a treaty signed originally signed on October 5, 1961, which allows for the simplified certification of notarized documents without full legalization

infringement
use by one party of intellectual property (such as copyright, trademark or patent) belonging to another party that causes damage to the rightful owner of the intellectual property

intellectual property	also referred to as "industrial property," it is an area of law that includes such assets as patents, trademarks and copyrights
International Patent Classification (IPC)	a system used by most countries in classifying their patent documents
Internet	a global computer network
Lanham Act[1]	current version of the U.S. trademark law originally enacted on July 5, 1946
legalization	administrative procedure to make a document legally acceptable for filing in a foreign jurisdiction
license	a legal agreement granting someone permission to use an intellectual property for certain purposes and under certain conditions

---

1. *15 U.S.C.S § 1051*

Madrid Protocol

a Protocol to the Madrid Agreement, which was adopted in 1989 and provides for the filing of international applications at the same time as the filing for the home national application. It also provides for the conversion of an international application into a national application if the home registration fails within the first five years.

Madrid Agreement Concerning the International Registration of Marks

a treaty originally signed in 1891, which offers trademark registration in various countries through a single application

Manual of Patent Examining Procedure (MPEP)

a manual published by the U.S. Patent and Trademark Office. It is a guide to the patent practices and procedures of the U.S. Patent and Trademark Office.

moral rights

the non-economic rights that an artist acquires by the simple act of creating a work of art. "Moral" rights are rights that either affect or have the potential to affect the artist's personality and reputation.

nonobviousness

one of the prerequisites to receiving a patent. The invention must be original and not obvious to others who work or are otherwise competent in a particular field of knowledge.

office action	an official written communication by a governmental body on the merits of an application
Paris Convention for the Protection of Industrial Property	a treaty originally signed in 1883. Among other requirements, the Paris Convention requires member nations to recognize a "priority filing date" of an application that is first filed in a home country
Patent Cooperation Treaty (PCT)	a treaty concluded in 1970, it established centralized filing procedures for international patent applications and standardized the application format
patent	a right granted by the government of a country that excludes other parties from making, using or selling an invention. The current United States Patent statutes provide for the protection of utility, plant, and design patents
power of attorney	a written authorization by one party known as a donor (such as an applicant) to an agent (such as an attorney) which allows the agent to act on behalf of the donor
prior art	any existing patents or patent applications or any other publication throughout the world, relevant to an invention

priority   the benefit of an earlier filing
                                      date. A request for a priority
                                      date may be made by an
                                      applicant of a patent or
                                      trademark application within 12
                                      months of the filing of another
                                      application for the same
                                      invention or trademark in
                                      another country

prosecution   the steps involved in following
                                      an application through to
                                      registration

provisional application   a temporary patent filing allowed
                                      in the United States to give the
                                      inventor priority rights allowed
                                      to inventors outside the United
                                      States

publication   a public notice issued by a
                                      governmental body after an
                                      application has received
                                      preliminary governmental
                                      approval. This notice allows
                                      interested party who feels final
                                      registration would adversely
                                      effect their own intellectual
                                      property rights the opportunity
                                      to file notice with the
                                      governmental body objecting to
                                      the final registration.

Registration   the granting of formal
                                      recognition of an intellectual
                                      property rights by a national
                                      government

right to publicity	the right of every human being to control the commercial use of his or her identity and likeness
search	an investigation conducted to determine if any type of intellectual property belongs to another party
service mark	any word, name, symbol or device, or any combination thereof that is used by a manufacturer or merchant to identify its services and to distinguish them from the services of others
trade secret	information, particularly competitive information, that is held secret by businesses
trade name	the name under which a company chooses to operate. A trade name is not necessarily a trademark
Trade Related Intellectual Property Issues (TRIPS)	an international agreement whose provisions affect international patent and trademark prosecution, protection and maintenance
trademark	any word, name, symbol or device, or any combination thereof that is used by a manufacturer or merchant to identify its products (or tangible goods) and to distinguish them from the products of others

Trademark Manual of Examining Procedure (TMEP)

a manual published by the U.S. Patent and Trademark Office. It is a guide to the trademark practices and procedures of the U.S. Patent and Trademark Office

Universal Copyright Convention (UCC)

a copyright treaty established in 1952 in Geneva, Switzerland. It is administered by UNESCO, a United Nations agency

World Intellectual Property Organization (WIPO)

an organization based in Geneva, Switzerland, which is concerned with the international protection and enforcement of intellectual property

Table 1

RECOMMENDED READING
AND REFERENCE

Compiled by
Charles K. Crider, Esq.

The following reference materials are provided as a foundation for researching intellectual property law. In addition, the materials serve as useful guides for those seeking essential information on the drafting of documents and the related prosecution procedures. For your convenience, the materials are categorized into the various areas of intellectual property. As this collection of materials is hardly extensive, you should contact the listed publishers or reference librarians to obtain additional materials.

PATENT REFERENCE MATERIALS

General Research

Brantley, Patricia N., *Patent Law Handbook*. (Clark Boardman Callaghan, 1996-97).

Chisum, Donald S., *Patents*. (Matthew Bender & Co., Inc., 1997).

Rosenberg, Peter D., *Patent Law Fundamentals*. (2nd Edition, Clark Boardman Callaghan, 1997).

Registration Procedure

Hawes, James E., *Patent Application Practice*. (2nd Edition, Clark Boardman Callaghan, 1994*)*.

Sheldon, Jeffrey G., *How To Write A Patent Application*. (Practising Law Institute, 1996).

Registration Forms

Brufsky, Allen D., and Kramer, Barry, *Patent Law Practice Forms.* (Clark Boardman Callaghan, 1997).

Horwitz, Lester, *Patent Office Rules and Practice: Forms.* (Matthew Bender & Co., Inc., 1997).

Patent Rules of Practice

37 C.F.R. 1

Crowne, James D., *Patent, Trademark, and Copyright Regulations.* BNA Books. Stock Numbers 1045 (10/96 Supp.); 1046. (Complete Set).

Horwitz, Lester, *Patent Office Rules and Practice.* (Matthew Bender & Co., Inc., 1997).

Manual of Patent Examining Procedure (MPEP). (United States Government Printing Office, 1996).

International Patent Practice

Jacobs, Alan J., *Patents Throughout the World.* (4th Edition, Clark Boardman Callaghan, 1997).

Litigation

Dunner, Donald R.; Gholz, Charles L.; Kakes, Michael J.; Hutchinson, George E., *Court of Appeals for the Federal Circuit: Practice & Procedure.* (Matthew Bender & Co., Inc., 1997).

Feinber, Dana Karen, and Russell, Kevin L., *Federal Circuit Patent Case Digest.* (Clark Boardman Callaghan, 1997).

Horwitz, Ethan, and Horwitz, Lester, *Patent Litigation and Practice.* (Matthew Bender & Co., Inc., 1997).

Licensing

Einhorn, Harold, *Patent Licensing Transactions*. (Matthew Bender & Co., Inc., 1997).

TRADEMARK REFERENCE MATERIALS

General Research

McCarthy, J. Thomas, *McCarthy on Trademarks and Unfair Competition*. (4th Edition, Clark Boardman Callaghan, 1997).

Registration Procedure

Hawes, James E., *Trademark Registration Practice*. (Clark Boardman Callaghan, 1997).

International Trademark Association (INTA), *State Trademark and Unfair Competition Law*. [International Trademark Association (INTA), 1997].

Gundersen, Glenn, *Trademark Searching: A Practical Guide to the Clearance of New Marks in the United States*. [International Trademark Association (INTA), 1995].

Registration Forms

Brufsky, Allen D., and Kramer, Barry, *Trademark Law Practice Forms*. (2nd Edition, Clark Boardman Callaghan, 1997).

Trademark Rules of Practice

37 C.F.R. 2

Crowne, James D., *Patent, Trademark, and Copyright Regulations*. [BNA Books. Stock Numbers 1045 (10/96 Supp.); 1046, 1996].

Trademark Manual of Examining Procedure (TMEP). (2nd Edition). (Government Printing Office, 1996).

International Registration Practice

Olsen, John R., and Maniatis, Spyros M., *Trademarks: World Law and Practice.* (FT Law & Tax, 1996).

Politi, Jeanine M., *Trademarks Throughout the World.* (4th Edition, Clark Boardman Callaghan, 1997).

A professional directory follows the text of this book, listing agents and attorneys practicing in patent and trademark law.

COPYRIGHT REFERENCE MATERIALS

General Research

Nimmer, David, and Nimmer, Melville B. *Nimmer on Copyright.* (Matthew Bender & Co. Inc., 1997).

Abrams, Howard B., *The Law of Copyright.* (Clark Boardman Callaghan, 1997).

Registration Procedure

Hawes, James E., *Copyright Registration Practice.* (Clark Boardman Callaghan, 1997).

Hazard Jr., John W., *Copyright Law In Business and Practice* (Warren, Gorham & Lamont, 1997).

Copyright Rules of Practice

37 C.F.R 201

Crowne, James D., *Patent, Trademark, and Copyright Regulations.* BNA Books. Stock Numbers 1045 (10/96 Supp.); 1046.

Compendium of Copyrights. (United States Government Printing Office).

International Copyright Practice

Geller, Paul Edward, and Nimmer, Melville B., *International Copyright Law and Practice*. (Matthew Bender & Co., Inc., 1997).

INTERNET/MULTIMEDIA LAW REFERENCE MATERIALS

Bender, David, *Computer Law: Software Protection*. (Matthew Bender & Co. Inc., 1997).

Louwers, Ernst-Jan, and Prins, Prof. Corien E.J., *International Computer Law*. (Matthew Bender & Co. Inc., 1996).

McCarthy, J. Thomas, *The Rights of Publicity and Privacy*. (Clark Boardman Callaghan, 1997).

Nimmer, Raymond T., *Information Law*. (Warren, Gorham, & Lamont, 1997).

Scott, Michael D., *Scott On Multimedia Law*. (2nd Edition, Aspen Law & Business, 1997).

Smedinghoff, Thomas J., *Multimedia Legal Handbook, A Guide From The Software Publishers Association*. (Wiley Law Publications, 1996).

TRADE SECRETS REFERENCE MATERIALS

Milgrim, Roger M., *Milgrim On Trade Secrets*. (Matthew Bender & Co. Inc., 1997).

PUBLISHING CONTACTS

Aspen Law & Business
c/o Aspen Publishers, Inc.
7201 McKinney Circle
Frederick, MD 21701
(800) 901-9074

BNA Books
1250 23rd St. N.W.
Washington, DC 20037-1165
(800) 960-1220

Clark Boardman Callaghan
155 Pfingsten Road
Deerfield, IL 60015
(800) 323-1336

**International Trademark
Association (INTA)**
1133 Avenue of the Americas
New York, NY 10036-6710
(212) 768-9887

Practising Law Institute
810 7th Avenue
New York, NY 10019
(800) 260-4754

Warren, Gorham & Lamont
31 St. James Avenue
Boston, MA 02116
(800) 950-1205

FT Law & Tax
21-27 Lamb's Conduit Street
London WCIN 3 NJ England
+44 171 242 2548

Matthew Bender & Co., Inc.
2 Park Avenue 7th Floor
New York, NY 10016-5675
(800) 223-1940

**Superintendent of Documents
United States Government
Printing Office**
Customer Service Section SSOS
Washington, DC 20402

Wiley Law Publications
John Wiley & Sons, Inc.
One Wiley Drive
Somerset, NJ 08875
(800) 225-5945

Table 2

SIGNIFICANT INTERNATIONAL
CONVENTIONS RELATING TO
PATENT, TRADEMARK and COPYRIGHT

PLEASE NOTE[1]

Country	Paris Convention - Priority	Bern Convention- Copyright	Patent Cooperation Treaty	Hague Convention- Legalization
Afghanistan				Yes[2]
Albania	Yes[3] (*Stockholm txt*)		Yes	Yes
Algeria	Yes (*Stockholm txt*)			Yes
Andorra				Yes
Angola				Yes
Anguilla				Yes
Antigua				Yes
Argentina	Yes (*Stockholm txt*)			None Required
Armenia[4]			Yes	Yes
Aruba				None Required
Australia	Yes (*Stockholm txt*)	Yes[5]	Yes	None Required

1. *This chart is not to be considered a comprehensive listing of all international conventions and treaties relating to the international practice of patent, trademark and copyright law. Only four of the most significant treaties are represented. Other pertinent treaties and conventions exist, and each country should be thoroughly researched by the practitioner. The relevant laws of each country are constantly changing. The information contained herein is the best available at the time of publication and may not currently be in force.*

2. *The Hague Convention is an international treaty concerning the requirement to legalize documents for filing in countries outside the home country. It is designed to streamline the process of filing documents overseas by eliminating many of the steps involved with legalizing documents.*

3. *The Paris Convention allows a party to claim the original filing date of an application filed in the applicant's home country in an application filed in another member country if the subsequent application is filed within six months of the original filing in the home country.*

4. *Former USSR Madrid filings can now be re-registered in Armenia.*

5. *The full name of the Bern Convention is the International Convention for the Protection of Literary and Artistic Works. It has become known as the Bern Convention because it was established in Bern, Switzerland, in 1886. The basic purpose of the treaty is "for the protection of the rights of authors."*

Country	Paris Convention - Priority	Bern Convention- Copyright	Patent Cooperation Treaty	Hague Convention- Legalization
Azerbaijan	Yes (*Stockholm txt*)		Yes	Yes
Austria	Yes (*Stockholm txt*)	Yes	Yes	None Required
Bahamas, The	Yes (*Stockholm txt*)	Yes		None Required
Bahrain				Yes
Bangladesh	Yes (*Stockholm txt*)			Yes
Barbados	Yes (*Stockholm txt*)	Yes	Yes	Yes
Belarus	Yes (*Stockholm txt*)		Yes	Yes
Belgium (*Benelux*)	Yes (*Stockholm txt*)	Yes	Yes	None Required
Belize				Yes
Benin	Yes (*Stockholm txt*)		Yes	Yes
Bermuda				Yes
Bolivia	Yes (*Stockholm txt*)			Yes
Bophutatswana[6]				None Required
Bosnia-Herzegovina[7]			Yes	Yes
Botswana				None Required
Brazil	Yes (*Stockholm txt*)	Yes	Yes	Yes
British Virgin Islands				None Required
Brunei				Yes
Bulgaria	Yes (*Stockholm txt*)	Yes	Yes	Yes
Burkina Faso	Yes (*Stockholm txt*)	Yes	Yes	None Required

---

6. *Bophutatswana has formally dissolved its independent government within South Africa and has become repatriated with South Africa.*

7. *Former Yugoslavian Madrid filings can now be re-registered in Bosnia-Herzegovina.*

Country	Paris Convention - Priority	Bern Convention- Copyright	Patent Cooperation Treaty	Hague Convention- Legalization
Cambodia				Yes
Canada	Yes *(Stockholm txt)*[8]	Yes	Yes	None Required
Cayman Islands				Yes
Central African Republic	Yes *(Stockholm txt)*	Yes	Yes	None Required
Chad	Yes *(Stockholm txt)*		Yes	None Required
Chile	Yes *(Stockholm txt)*	Yes		Yes
China (People's Republic)	Yes *(Stockholm txt)*		Yes	Yes
Colombia	Yes *(Stockholm txt)*	Yes		Yes
Congo	Yes *(Stockholm txt)*	Yes	Yes	Yes
Costa Rica	Yes *(Stockholm txt)*	Yes		Yes
Cote d'Ivoire (*Ivory Coast*)	Yes *(Stockholm txt)*	Yes	Yes	Yes
Croatia	Yes *(Stockholm txt)*			Yes
Cuba	Yes *(Stockholm txt)*		Yes	Yes
Cyprus	Yes *(Stockholm txt)*	Yes		None Required
Czech Republic	Yes *(Stockholm txt)*	Yes	Yes	None Required
Denmark	Yes *(Stockholm txt)*	Yes	Yes	None Required
Dominica				Yes
Dominican Republic	Yes *(Hauge txt)*			Yes

8. *The Canadian Trade Marks Office* **no longer requires** *the filing of a certified copy of the parent application as filed to maintain the claim of priority.*

Country	Paris Convention - Priority	Bern Convention- Copyright	Patent Cooperation Treaty	Hague Convention- Legalization
Ecuador				Yes
Egypt	Yes (*Stockholm txt*)	Yes		Yes
El Salvador	Yes (*Stockholm txt*)			Yes
Estonia	Yes (*Stockholm txt*)		Yes	Yes
Falkland Islands				Yes
Fiji		Yes		Yes
Finland	Yes (*Stockholm txt*)	Yes	Yes	None Required
France	Yes (*Stockholm txt*)	Yes	Yes	None Required
French Polynesia (*Covered by registrations in France*)				
Gabon	Yes (*Stockholm txt*)	Yes	Yes	Yes
Gambia				None Required
Georgia	Yes (*Stockholm txt*)		Yes	None Required
Germany	Yes (*Stockholm txt*)[9]	Yes	Yes	None Required
Ghana				None Required
Gibraltar				Yes
Greece	Yes (*Stockholm txt*)	Yes	Yes	None Required
Grenada				Yes
Guatemala				Yes
Guernsey				Yes
Guinea	Yes (*Stockholm txt*)	Yes	Yes	Yes
Guinea-Bissau	Yes (*Stockholm txt*)			Yes

9. *The copy of the basic U.S. application required to maintain the claim of priority **does not** need to be certified.*

Country	Paris Convention - Priority	Bern Convention- Copyright	Patent Cooperation Treaty	Hague Convention- Legalization
Guyana				Yes
Haiti	Yes (*Stockholm txt*)			Yes
Holy See	Yes (*Stockholm txt*)	Yes		Yes
Honduras				Yes
Hong Kong				None Required
Hungary	Yes (*Stockholm txt*)	Yes	Yes	None Required
Iceland	Yes (*Stockholm txt*)	Yes	Yes	None Required
India		Yes		Yes
Indonesia	Yes (*Stockholm txt*)			Yes
Iran	Yes (*Stockholm txt*)			Yes
Iraq	Yes (*Stockholm txt*)			Yes
Ireland	Yes (*Stockholm txt*)	Yes	Yes	None Required
Israel	Yes (*Stockholm txt*)	Yes	Yes	None Required
Italy	Yes (*Stockholm txt*)		Yes	None Required
Jamaica				None Required
Japan	Yes (*Stockholm txt*)	Yes	Yes	None Required
Jersey				Yes
Jordan[10]	Yes (*Stockholm txt*)			Yes
Kazakhstan	Yes (*Stockholm txt*)		Yes	None Required

---

10. *Effective May 1996, Jordan has eliminated the requirement to submit an Israeli Boycott questionnaire as a prerequisite to obtaining a Jordanian Registration. This ends filings that have prohibited most foreign registrations over the preceding forty years.*

Country	Paris Convention - Priority	Bern Convention- Copyright	Patent Cooperation Treaty	Hague Convention- Legalization
Kenya	Yes (Stockholm txt)		Yes	None Required
Kiribati				Yes
Korea	Yes (Stockholm txt)		Yes	None Required
Kuwait				Yes
Kyrgyzstan	Yes (Stockholm txt)		Yes	Yes
Laos				Yes
Latvia	Yes (Stockholm txt)		Yes	None Required
Lebanon	Yes (Stockholm txt)	Yes		Yes
Lesotho[11]	Yes (Stockholm txt)		Yes	None Required
Liberia			Yes	Yes
Libya	Yes (Stockholm txt)	Yes		Yes
Liechtenstein	Yes (Stockholm txt)	Yes	Yes	None Required
Lithuania	Yes (Stockholm txt)			None Required
Luxembourg (Benelux)	Yes (Stockholm txt)	Yes	Yes	None Required
Macao[12]				Yes
Macedonia	Yes (Stockholm txt)		Yes	None Required
Madagascar	Yes (Stockholm txt)	Yes	Yes	Yes
Malagasy Republic				Yes

---

11. *Lesotho has formally dissolved its independent government within South Africa and has become repatriated with South Africa.*

12. *Macao is currently under Portuguese administration but will return to the People's Republic of China in December 1999. Any applications filed between December 31, 1987, and before December 31, 1999, will be prosecuted independently in Macao with triple fees applicable. The register will be dissolved in 1999.*

Country	Paris Convention - Priority	Bern Convention-Copyright	Patent Cooperation Treaty	Hague Convention-Legalization
Malawi	Yes (*Stockholm txt*)		Yes	None Required
Malaysia	Yes (*Stockholm txt*)			Yes
Malta	Yes (*Stockholm txt*)	Yes		Yes
Mauritius	Yes (*Stockholm txt*)	Yes	Yes	None Required
Mexico	Yes (*Stockholm txt*)	Yes	Yes	Yes
Moldova	Yes (*Stockholm txt*)		Yes	None Required
Monaco	Yes (*Stockholm txt*)	Yes	Yes	None Required
Mongolia	Yes (*Stockholm txt*)		Yes	Yes
Montserrat				Yes
Morocco	Yes (*Stockholm txt*)	Yes		None Required
Namibia				None Required
Nepal				None Required
Netherlands (*Benelux*)	Yes (*Stockholm txt*)	Yes	Yes	None Required
Netherlands Antilles	Yes (*Stockholm txt*)			None Required
New Zealand	Yes (*Stockholm txt*)	Yes	Yes	Yes
Nicaragua				Yes
Niger	Yes (*Stockholm txt*)	Yes	Yes	Yes
Nigeria	Yes (*Lisbon txt*)			None Required

Country	Paris Convention - Priority	Bern Convention- Copyright	Patent Cooperation Treaty	Hague Convention- Legalization
Norway	Yes (*Stockholm txt*)	Yes	Yes	None Required
AIPO[13] African Union)	Yes (*Stockholm txt*)	Yes	Yes	None Required
Oman				Yes
Pakistan		Yes		Yes
Panama	Yes (*Stockholm txt*)			Yes
Papua New Guinea				None Required
Paraguay				Yes
Peru	Yes (*Stockholm txt*)			Yes
Philippines[14]	Yes (*Stockholm txt*)	Yes		Yes
Poland	Yes (*Stockholm txt*)		Yes	Yes
Portugal[15]	Yes (*Stockholm txt*)	Yes	Yes	None Required
Puerto Rico	Yes (*Stockholm txt*			None Required
Qatar				Yes (*translation into Arabic required*)
Reunion (*Covered by registrations in France*)				
Romania	Yes (*Stockholm txt*)	Yes	Yes	Yes
Russian Federation (*Formerly U.S.S.R*)			Yes	None Required

13. *Member countries of the AIPO are Benin, Burkina Faso, Cameroon, Central African Republic, Chad, Congo, Djihourti, Gabon, Guinea, Ivory Coast, Mali, Mauritania, Niger, Senegal and Togo. A registration in one member country is automatically valid in all member countries.*

14. *A trademark application in the Philippines must be based either on (1) a foreign application/registration or (2) actual use in the Philippines for at least two months prior to filing.*

15. *A new trademark law became effective June 1, 1995. The opposition period is now two months. Late renewals are **no longer possible** for marks registered under the new law.*

Country	Paris Convention - Priority	Bern Convention- Copyright	Patent Cooperation Treaty	Hague Convention- Legalization
Rwanda	Yes (*Stockholm txt*)	Yes		Yes
Saint Helena				Yes
Saint Kitts and Nevis	Yes (*Stockholm txt*)			Yes
Saint Lucia	Yes (*Stockholm txt*)		Yes	Yes
Saint Vincent and the Grenadines				Yes
Saudi Arabia				Yes
Senegal	Yes (*Stockholm txt*)		Yes	Yes
Seychelles				None Required
Singapore	Section 75 of Singapore Trade Marks Act[16]		Yes	Yes
Slovakia (Slovak Republic)	Yes (*Stockholm txt*)		Yes	None Required
Slovenia	Yes (*Stockholm txt*)		Yes	None Required
Solomon Islands				Yes
Somalia				Yes
South Africa	Yes (*Stockholm txt*)	Yes		None Required
Spain	Yes (*Stockholm txt*)	Yes	Yes	None Required
Sri Lanka (*formerly Ceylon*)	Yes (*Stockholm txt*)	Yes	Yes	Yes
Sudan	Yes (*Hague txt*)		Yes	Yes[17]

16. Although Singapore is not yet a member of the Paris Convention, Section 75 of the Trade Marks Act grants priority to trademark applications from numerous counties. However, effective March 1, 1991, Section 75 was amended to **eliminate** priority claims made on the basis of the filing of applications in the United Kingdom, Australia, Canada, Sri Lanka, Zambia, Zimbabwe, New Zealand and Malawi.

17. All documents filed in Sudan must be submitted in Arabic or be accompanied by an Arabic translation.

Country	Paris Convention - Priority	Bern Convention- Copyright	Patent Cooperation Treaty	Hague Convention- Legalization
Suriname	Yes (*Stockholm txt*)	Yes		None Required
Swaziland	Yes (*Stockholm txt*)		Yes	None Required
Sweden	Yes (*Stockholm txt*)	Yes	Yes	None Required
Switzerland	Yes (*Stockholm txt*)	Yes	Yes	None Required
Syria				Yes
Tadjikistan			Yes	Yes
Taiwan (Republic of China)				Yes
Tanganyika	Yes (*Stockholm txt*)			Yes
Tanzania				Yes
Thailand		Yes		Yes
Togo	Yes (*Stockholm txt*)	Yes	Yes	Yes
Tonga				Yes
Trinidad and Tobago	Yes (*Stockholm txt*)		Yes	Yes
Tunisia	Yes (*Stockholm txt*)	Yes		Yes
Turkey	Yes (*Stockholm txt*)	Yes	Yes	Yes
Turkmenistan	Yes (*Stockholm txt*)		Yes	Yes
Tuvalu				Yes
Uganda	Yes (*Stockholm txt*)		Yes	None Required
United Kingdom (*including certain British Territories and Palestine*)	Yes (*Stockholm txt*)	Yes	Yes	None Required

Country	Paris Convention - Priority	Bern Convention- Copyright	Patent Cooperation Treaty	Hague Convention- Legalization
United Arab Emirates[18]	Yes (*Stockholm txt*)			Yes
United States	Yes (*Stockholm txt*)	Yes	Yes	None Required
Uruguay	Yes (*Stockholm txt*)			Yes
Uzbekistan	Yes (*Stockholm txt*)		Yes	Yes
Vanautu				Yes
Venda[19]				Yes
Venezuela	Yes (*Stockholm txt*)	Yes		Yes
Vietnam	Yes (*Stockholm txt*)		Yes	None Required
Yugoslavia[20]	Yes (*Stockholm txt*)	Yes		None Required
Zaire	Yes (*Stockholm txt*)	Yes		Yes
Zambia	Yes (*Stockholm txt*)			Yes
Zimbabwe	Yes (*Stockholm txt*)	Yes		Yes

18. *The United Arab Emirates (U.A.E.) is a federation of the Emirates of Abu-Dhabi, Ajman, Dubai, Fujairah, Ras Al-Khaimah, Sharjah, and Umm Al-Qaiwain. Prior to January 1993, only Ras Al-Khaimah had formally enacted a trademark law. A new trademark law came into effect in the U.A.E. on January 12, 1993. The Implementing Regulations for the new law was issued under Ministerial Decision No. 6 for 1993 on February 2, 1993. Currently, there remains no trademark protection in the Emirates of Bhutan, Maldives and Myanmar. The only form of protection available in these Emirates is the publication of Cautionary Notices.*

19. *Venda has formally dissolved its independent government within South Africa and has become repatriated with South Africa.*

20. *Yugoslavia no longer exists as an independent political entity, as Croatia, Slovenia, Bosnia, Herzegovina and Macedonia have declared their independence beginning in July 1992. On April 7, 1992, the Federal Republic of Yugoslavia was reestablished comprising Serbia and Montenegro. Currently, no trademark prosecution occurs in this new republic, and the U.S. has placed an embargo on all payments, including trademark fees, to the new republic.*

Table 3

UNITED STATES PATENT AND TRADEMARK FEES AS OF OCTOBER 1, 1997[1]

- 37 C.F.R. Section - Description	- Fee

PATENTS

1.16(a)
Basic filing fee – utility .... 790.00 / 395.00[2]

1.16(b)
Independent claims in excess of three................................. 82.00 / 41.00

1.16(c)
Claims in excess of twenty .... 22.00 / 11.00

1.16(d)
Multiple dependent claim .... 270.00 / 135.00

1.16(e)
Surcharge – Late filing fee or oath or declaration .... 130.00 / 65.00

1.16(f)
Design filing fee .... 330.00 / 165.00

1.16(g)
Plant filing fee .... 540.00 / 270.00

1.16(h)
Reissue filing fee .... 790.00 / 395.00

---

1. New and updated patent and trademark fees are made effective on October 1 of each year.

2. The second fee quoted a small entity fee. As mentioned in Chapter 2, individual inventors, small businesses, universities and non-profit organizations are classified as "small entities" and qualify for a fifty percent (50%) discount on the fees.

1.16(i)
Reissue independent claims over original patent .... 82.00 / 41.00

1.16(j)
Reissue claims in excess of 20 and
over original patent .... 22.00 / 11.00

1.16(k)
Provisional application filing fee .... 150.00 / 75.00

1.16(l)
Surcharge – Late provisional filing fee or cover sheet .... 50.00 /25.00

1.17(k)
Non-English specification 130.00

PATENT ISSUE FEES

1.18(a)
Utility issue fee ....1,320.00 / 660.00

1.18(b)
Design issue fee .... 450.00 / 225.00

1.18(c)
Plant issue fee .... 670.00 / 335.00

PATENT MAINTENANCE FEES
Applications Filed on or after December 12, 1980

1.20(e)
Due at 3.5 years ....1,050.00 / 525.00

1.20(f)
Due at 7.5 years .... 2,100.00 / 1,050.00

1.20(g)
Due at 11.5 years .... 3,160.00 / 1,580.00

1.20(h)
Surcharge – Late payment within 6 months .... 130.00 / 65.00

1.20(i)(1)
Surcharge after expiration –
Late payment is unavoidable 700.00

1.20(i)(2)
Surcharge after expiration –
Late payment is unintentional 1,640.00

MISCELLANEOUS PATENT FEES

1.20(j)(1)
Extension of term of patent..1,120.00

1.20(j)(2)
Initial application for interim extension[3] 420.00

1.20(j)(3)
Subsequent application for interim extension[4] 220.00

1.17(n)
Requesting publication of SIR –
Prior to examiner action ....920.00[5]*

1.17(o)
Requesting publication of SIR –
After examiner action 1,840.00*

1.17(r)
For filing a submission after final rejection .... 790.00 / 395.00

1.17(s)
For each additional invention to be examined .... 790.00 / 395.00

1.20(a)
Certificate of correction.. 100.00

1.20(c)
For filing a request for reexamination 2,520.00

---

3. *37 C.F.R. §1.790*
4. *37 C.F.R. §1.790*
5. *The fees marked with "*" are reduced by the basic filing fee*

1.20(d)
Statutory disclaimer .... 110.00 / 55.00

PATENT EXTENSION FEES

1.17(a)
Extension for response within first month.......................... 110.00 / 55.00

1.17(b)
Extension for response within second month .... 400.00 / 200.00

1.17(c)
Extension for response within third month........................ 950.00 / 475.00

1.17(d)
Extension for response within fourth month ....1,510.00 / 755.00

Extension for response within fifth month[6]................... 2,060.00 / 1,030.00

PATENT APPEALS/INTERFERENCE FEES

1.17(e)
Notice of appeal .... 310.00 / 155.00

1.17(f)
Filing a brief in support of an appeal .... 310.00 / 155.00

1.17(g)
Request for oral hearing... 270.00 / 135.00

PATENT PETITION FEES

N/A
Petitions to the Commissioner,
unless otherwise specified.. 130.00

1.17(p)
Submission of an Information Disclosure Statement........................ 240.00

---

6. *The rulemaking "**Changes to Patent Practice and Procedure**" will adopt in 1998 a fifth-month extension fee (37 C.F.R. §1.17(a)(5)), and change the designation of 37 C.F.R. § 1.17(a) through (g) to 37 C.F.R. § 1.17(a)(1) through (a)(4) and (b) through (d)*

1.17(j)
Petition to institute a public use proceeding.................................1,510.00

1.17(l)
Petition to revive unavoidably abandoned application .... 110.00 / 55.00

1.17(m)
Petition to revive unintentionally abandoned application.......1,320.00 / 660.00

1.17(q)
Petitions related to provisional applications 50.00

PATENT SERVICE FEES

1.19(a)(1)(i)
Printed copy of patent w/o color, regular service.............................. 3.00

1.19(a)(1)(ii)
Printed copy of patent w/o color, overnight delivery
to PTO box or overnight fax 6.00

1.19(a)(1)(iii)
Printed copy of patent w/o color, ordered via expedited mail or fax,
expedited service 25.00

1.19(a)(2)
Printed copy of plant patent, in color 15.00

1.19(a)(3)
Copy of utility patent or SIR, with color drawings 25.00

1.19(b)(1)(i)
Certified copy of patent application as filed, regular service.................15.00

1.19(b)(1)(ii)
Certified copy of patent application, expedited local service.................30.00

1.19(b)(2)
Certified or uncertified copy of patent-related
file wrapper and contents 150.00

1.19(b)(3)
Certified or uncertified copy of document,
unless otherwise provided...25.00

1.19(b)(4)
For assignment records, abstract of title
and certification, per patent 25.00

1.19(c)
Library service 50.00

1.19(d)
List of U.S. patents and SIRs in subclass 3.00

1.19(e)
Uncertified statement re status of maintenance fee payments 10.00

1.19(f)
Copy of non-U.S. document...25.00

1.19(g)
Comparing and certifying copies, per document, per copy...................25.00

1.19(h)
Additional filing receipt, duplicate or corrected due
to applicant error 25.00

1.21(c)
Filing a disclosure document 10.00

1.21(e)
International type search report 40.00

1.21(h)
Recording each patent assignment, agreement or
other paper, per property 40.00

1.21(i)
Publication in Official Gazette 25.00

PCT FEES – NATIONAL STAGE

1.492(e)
Oath or declaration after twenty or thirty months
from priority date ....130.00 / 65.00

1.492(f)
English translation after twenty or thirty months
from priority date 130.00

1.492(a)(4)
Claims meet PCT Article 33(1)-(4) – IPEA – U.S. .... 98.00 / 49.00

1.492(b)
Claims – extra independent (over three).............................. 82.00 / 41.00

1.492(c)
Claims – extra total (over twenty)..................................... 22.00 / 11.00

1.492(d)
Claims – multiple dependent .... 270.00 / 135.00

1.492(a)(5)
For filing with EPO or JPO search report .... 930.00 / 465.00

PCT FEES – INTERNATIONAL STAGE

1.445(a)(1)
Transmittal fee 240.00

1.445(a)(2)
PCT search fee – no U.S. application 700.00

1.445(a)(3)
Supplemental search per additional invention............................. 210.00

1.445(a)(2)
PCT search – prior U.S. application.. 450.00

1.482(a)(1)
Preliminary examination fee – ISA was the U.S. 490.00

1.482(a)(1)
Preliminary examination fee – ISA not the U.S. 750.00

1.482(a)(2)
Additional invention – ISA was the U.S. 140.00

1.482(a)(2)
Additional invention – ISA not the U.S. 270.00

- 37 C.F.R. SECTION
- DESCRIPTION   **- FEE**

TRADEMARKS

2.6(a)(1)
Application for registration, per class 245.00

2.6(a)(2)
Filing an Amendment to Allege Use under § 1(c), per class 100.00

2.6(a)(3)
Filing a Statement of Use under § 1(d)(1), per class 100.00

2.6(a)(4)
Filing a Request for a Six-month Extension of Time for
Filing a Statement of Use per class 100.00

2.6(a)(5)
Application for renewal, per class 300.00

2.6(a)(6)
Additional fee for late renewal, per class 100.00

2.6(a)(7)
Publication of mark under § 12(c), per class 100.00

2.6(a)(8)
Issuing new certificate of registration 100.00

2.6(a)(9)
Certificate of correction, registrants error 100.00

2.6(a)(10)
Filing disclaimer to registration...100.00

2.6(a)(11)
Filing amendment to registration 100.00

2.6(a)(12)
Filing § 8 affidavit, per class 100.00

2.6(a)(13)
Filing § 15 affidavit, per class 100.00

2.6(a)(14)
Filing combined §§ 8 & 15 affidavit, per class 200.00

2.6(a)(15)
Petition to the Commissioner...100.00

2.6(a)(16)
Petition for cancellation, per class...200.00

2.6(a)(17)
Notice of opposition, per class 200.00

2.6(a)(18)
Ex parte appeal, per class 100.00

2.6(a)(19)
Dividing an application, per new application
(file wrapper) created...100.00

TRADEMARK SERVICE FEES

2.6(b)(1)(i)
Printed copy of each registered mark, regular service 3.00

2.6(b)(1)(ii)
Printed copy of each registered mark,
overnight delivery to PTO box or overnight fax 6.00

2.6(b)(1)(iii)
Printed copy of each registered mark
ordered via expedited mail or
fax, expedited service 25.00

2.6(b)(4)(i)
Certified copy of registered mark, with title and/or status,
regular service 15.00

2.6(b)(4)(ii)
Certified copy of registered mark, with title and/or status,
expedited local service..30.00

2.6(b)(2)(i)
Certified copy of trademark application as filed,
regular service 15.00

2.6(b)(2)(ii)
Certified copy of trademark application as filed,
expedited local service..30.00

2.6(b)(3)
Certified or uncertified copy of trademark-related
file wrapper and contents 50.00

2.6(b)(5)
Certified or uncertified copy of trademark document,
unless otherwise provided...25.00

2.6(b)(7)
For assignment records, abstracts of title and certification
per registration..25.00

1.19(g)
Comparing and certifying copies, per document, per copy...................25.00

2.6(b)(9)
Self-service copy charge, per page 0.25

TRADEMARK ASSIGNMENT RECORDALS

2.6(b)(6)
Recording trademark assignment, agreement or other paper,
first mark per document..40.00

2.6(b)(6)
For second and subsequent marks in the same document 25.00

Table 4

PATENT AND TRADEMARK DEPOSITORY LIBRARIES AS OF JANUARY 1, 1997

Alabama
Auburn University:
Ralph Brown Draughon Library 334/ 844-1747

Birmingham:
Birmingham Public Library 205/ 226-3620

Alaska
Anchorage:
Z. J. Loussac Public Library,
Anchorage Municipal Libraries 907/ 562-7323

Arizona
Tempe:
Daniel E. Noble Science and Engineering Library/Science/Reference
Arizona State University 602/ 965-7010

Arkansas
Little Rock:
Arkansas State Library 501/ 682-2053

California
Los Angeles:
Los Angeles Public Library 213/ 228-7220

Sacramento:
California State Library 916/ 654-0069

San Diego:
San Diego Public Library 619/ 236-5813

San Francisco:
San Francisco Public Library 415/ 557-4500

Sunnyvale:
Sunnyvale Center for
Innovation, Invention & Ideas 408/ 730-7290

Colorado
Denver:
Denver Public Library 303/ 640-6220

Connecticut
New Haven:
Science Park Patent Library/
Technology Resource Center 203/ 786-5447

Delaware
Newark:
University of Delaware Library 302/ 831-2965

District of Columbia
Washington: Founders Library,
Howard University... 202/ 806-7252

Florida
Fort Lauderdale:
Broward County Main Library 954/ 357-7444

Miami:
Miami-Dade Public Library................................... 305/ 375-2665

Orlando:
University of Central Florida Libraries..................... 407/ 823-2562

Tampa:
Tampa Campus Library,
University of South Florida 813/ 974-2726

Georgia
Atlanta:
Library and Information Center,
Georgia Institute of Technology.............................. 404/ 894-4508

Hawaii
Honolulu:
Hawaii State Library 808/ 586-3477

Idaho
Moscow:
University of Idaho Library................................... 208/ 885-6235

Illinois
Chicago:
Chicago Public Library 312/ 747-4450

Springfield:
Illinois State Library.. 217/ 782-5659

Indiana
Indianapolis:
Indianapolis-Marion County Public Library 317/ 269-1741

West Lafayette:
Siegesmund Engineering Library,
Purdue University... 317/ 494-2872

Iowa
Des Moines:
State Library of Iowa... 515/ 281-4118

Kansas
Wichita:
Ablah Library, Wichita State University 316/ 978-3155

Kentucky
Louisville:
Louisville Free Public Library............................... 502/ 574-1611

Louisiana
Baton Rouge:
Troy H. Middleton Library,
Louisiana State University...................................... 504/ 388-5652

Maine
Orono:
Raymond H. Fogler Library,
University of Maine 207/ 581-1678

Maryland
College Park:
Engineering and Physical Sciences Library,
University of Maryland 301/ 405-9157

Massachusetts
Amherst:
Physical Sciences and Engineering Library,
University of Massachusetts................................... 413/ 545-1370

Boston:
Boston Public Library .... 617/ 536-5400 (x. 265)

Michigan
Ann Arbor:
Media Union Library,
The University of Michigan................................... 313/ 647-5735

Big Rapids:
Abigail S. Timme Library,
Ferris State University 616/ 592-3602

Detroit:
Great Lakes Patent and Trademark Center,
Detroit Public Library.. 313/ 833-3379

Minnesota
Minneapolis:
Minneapolis Public Library & Information Center 612/ 372-6570

Mississippi
Jackson:
Mississippi Library Commission 601/ 359-1036

Missouri
Kansas City:
Linda Hall Library 816/ 363-4600

St. Louis:
St. Louis Public Library .... 314/ 241-2288 (x. 390)

Montana
Butte:
University of Montana Library 406/ 496-4281

Nebraska
Lincoln:
Engineering Library,
Nebraska Hall 402/ 472-3411

Nevada
Reno:
University of Nevada-Reno .... 702/ 784-6500 (x. 257)

New Hampshire
Concord:
New Hampshire State Library 603/ 271-2239

New Jersey
Newark:
Newark Public Library 201/ 733-7782

Piscataway:
Library of Science and Medicine,
Rutgers University 908/ 445-2895

New Mexico
Albuquerque:
Centennial Science and Engineering Library,
The University of New Mexico 505/ 277-4412

New York
Albany:
New York State Library,
Science, Industry and Business Library..................... 518/ 474-5355

Buffalo:
Buffalo and Erie County Public Library.................... 716/ 858-7101

New York City:
Science, Industry and Business Library..................... 212/ 592-7000

North Carolina
Raleigh:
D. H. Hill Library,
North Carolina State University.............................. 919/ 515-3280

North Dakota
Grand Forks:
Chester Fritz Library,
University of North Dakota 701/ 777-4888

Ohio
Akron:
Akron-Summit County Public Library 330/ 643-9075

Cincinnati:
The Public Library of Cincinnati
and Hamilton County... 513/ 369-6936

Cleveland:
Cleveland Public Library 216/ 623-2870

Columbus:
Ohio State University Libraries 614/ 292-6175

Toledo:
Toledo/Lucas County Public Library 419/ 259-5212

Oklahoma
Stillwater:
Oklahoma State University.................................... 405/ 744-7086

Oregon
Portland:
Paul L. Boley Law Library,
Lewis & Clark College 503/ 768-6786

Pennsylvania
Philadelphia:
The Free Library of Philadelphia 215/ 686-5331

Pittsburgh:
The Carnegie Library of Pittsburgh 412/ 622-3138

University Park:
Pattee Library
Pennsylvania State University 814/ 865-4861

Puerto Rico
Mayagüez:
General Library,
University of Puerto Rico .... 787/ 832-4040 (x. 3459)

Rhode Island
Providence:
Providence Public Library..................................... 401/ 455-8027

South Carolina
Clemson:
R. M. Cooper Library,
Clemson University.. 864/ 656-3024

South Dakota
Rapid City:
Devereaux Library,
South Dakota School of
Mines and Technology 605/ 394-6822

Tennessee
Memphis:
Memphis & Shelby County Public Library
and Information Center 901/ 725-8877

Nashville:
Stevenson Science and
Engineering Library, Vanderbilt University 615/ 322-2717

Texas
Austin:
McKinney Engineering Library,
The University of Texas at Austin 512/ 495-4500

College Station:
Sterling C. Evans Library,
Texas A&M University 409/ 845-3826

Dallas:
Dallas Public Library 214/ 670-1468

Houston:
The Fondren Library,
Rice University .... 713/ 527-8101 (x. 2587)

Utah
Salt Lake City:
Marriott Library,
University of Utah 801/ 581-8394

Vermont
Burlington:
Bailey/Howe Library,
University of Vermont .... (not open as of April 1997)

Virginia
Richmond:
James Branch Cabell Library,
Virginia Commonwealth University 804/ 828-1104

Washington
Seattle:
Engineering Library,
University of Washington 206/ 543-0740

West Virginia
Morgantown:
Evansdale Library,
West Virginia University .... 304/ 293-2510 (x. 113)

Wisconsin
Madison:
Kurt F. Wendt Library,
University of Wisconsin-Madison............................ 608/ 262-6845

Milwaukee:
Milwaukee Public Library..................................... 414/ 286-3051

Wyoming
Casper:
Natrona County Public Library 307/ 237-4935

Table 5

HAGUE CONVENTION MEMBERS
AS OF JUNE 1996

Antigua & Barbuda	Marshall Islands
Argentina	Mauritius
Armenia	Mexico
Australia	The Netherlands *(Including*
Austria	*The Netherlands Antilles)*
The Bahamas	Norway
Belgium	Panama
Belize	Portugal
Bosnia/Herzegovina	Russia
Botswana	San Marino
Belarus	Seychelles
Croatia	Slovenia
Cyprus	South Africa
El Salvador	Spain
Fiji	Suriname
Finland	Swaziland
France *(Including*	Switzerland
French Guyana	Tonga
Guadeloupe	Turkey
Martinique	United Kingdom
Reunion	United States
Dijouti	Yugoslavia
New Hebrides	
Comoro Island	
French Polynesia	
New Caledonia	
St. Pierre & Miquelon	
Wallis & Futuna)	

Additional information, including a text of the Convention, can be obtained by contacting the following:

Permanent Bureau
Hague Conference on Private International Law
6, Scheveningseweg
2517 KT   Fax: (70) 360-4867
The Hague, The Netherlands   Phone: (70) 363-3303

Table 6

INDEX OF WEBSITES RELEVANT TO INTELLECTUAL PROPERTY PRACTICE

Basic Search Engines

http://www.metacrawler.com:80/.......................................
METACRAWLER SEARCHING

http://www.excite.com/ ....
EXCITE WEB SEARCHING

http://dialog.krinfo.com/ ....
DIALOG (KNIGHT-RIDDER) WEB

http://www.four11.com/...
FOUR11 DIRECTORY SERVICES FOR INDIVIDUALS

http://www.infospace.com/ ....
INFOSPACE DIRECTORY

Search Resources for Additional Information

http://www.tollfree.att.net/ ....
AT&T TOLL-FREE INTERNET DIRECTORY

http://www.bmi.com/ ....
BMI HOME PAGE

http://www.ucc.ie/info/net/acronyms/index.html ....
ACRONYM AND ABBREVIATION LIST

http://www.matisse.net:80/files/glossary.html ....
GLOSSARY OF INTERNET TERMS

http://rs.internic.net/cgi-bin/whois ....
INTERNIC INTERFACE TO WHOIS

http://www.lawguru.com/...
LAWGURU.COM

http://www.adage.com/..
ADVERTISING AGE WEBSITE

Government Sites

http://www.uspto.gov/ ....
UNITED STATES PATENT AND TRADEMARK OFFICE
http://www.barlinc.org./appeals.html..................................
UNITED STATES COURT OF APPEALS OPINIONS
http://www.nara.gov/nara/fedreg/fedreg.html ....
OFFICE OF THE FEDERAL REGISTER
http://thomas.loc.gov/home/thomas.html ....
THOMAS – U.S. CONGRESS ON THE INTERNET

Patent Trademark and Copyright Specific Sites

http://www.thomson-thomson.com/ ....
THOMSON & THOMSON SERVICES
http://patent.womplex.ibm.com:80/advquery.html.................
PATENT SERVER: ADVANCED TEXT SEARCH
http://www.smartpatents.com/ ....
SMARTPATENTS HOME PAGE
http://www.micropat.com/..
MICROPATENT
http://www.copyright.com:80/ ....
COPYRIGHT CLEARANCE CENTER
http://www.questel.orbit.com/patents/patres.html..................
QUESTEL-ORBIT: PATENT AND TRADEMARK RESOURCES
http://www.law.cornell.edu/lanham/lanham.table.html ....
LANHAM ACT
http://bel.avonibp.co.uk:80/bricolage/resources/lounge/
bureau/copyright/index.html..................................
COPYRIGHT OFFICE
http://plaza.interport.net/inta/index.html ....
INTERNATIONAL TRADEMARK ASSOCIATION (INTA)

Table 7

UNITED STATES PATENT CLASSIFICATIONS

Class Plt - Plants
Class 2 - Apparel
Class 4 - Baths, Closets, Sinks, and Spittoons
Class 5 - Beds
Class 7 - Compound Tools
Class 8 - Bleaching and Dyeing; Fluid Treatment and Chemical Modification of Textiles
Class 12 - Boot and Shoe Making
Class 14 - Bridges
Class 15 - Brushing, Scrubbing, and General Cleaning
Class 16 - Miscellaneous Hardware
Class 19 - Textiles: Fiber Preparation
Class 23 - Chemistry: Physical Processes
Class 24 - Buckles, Buttons, Clasps, Etc.
Class 26 - Textiles: Cloth Finishing
Class 27 - Undertaking
Class 28 - Textiles: Manufacturing
Class 29 - Metal Working
Class 30 - Cutlery
Class 33 - Geometrical Instruments
Class 34 - Drying and Gas or Vapor Contact with Solids
Class 36 - Boots, Shoes, and Leggings
Class 37 - Excavating
Class 38 - Textiles: Ironing or Smoothing
Class 40 - Card, Picture, or Sign Exhibiting
Class 42 - Firearms
Class 43 - Fishing, Trapping, and Vermin Destroying
Class 44 - Fuel and Related Compositions
Class 47 - Plant Husbandry
Class 48 - Gas: Heating and Illuminating
Class 49 - Movable or Removable Closures
Class 51 - Abrading
Class 52 - Static Structures (e.g., Buildings)
Class 53 - Package Making
Class 54 - Harness
Class 55 - Gas Separation
Class 56 - Harvesters
Class 57 - Textiles: Spinning, Twisting, and Twining
Class 59 - Chain, Staple, and Horseshoe Making
Class 60 - Power Plants
Class 62 - Refrigeration
Class 63 - Jewelry
Class 65 - Glass Manufacturing
Class 66 - Textiles: Knitting
Class 68 - Textiles: Fluid Treating Apparatus
Class 69 - Leather Manufactures

Class 70 - Locks
Class 71 - Chemistry: Fertilizers
Class 72 - Metal Deforming
Class 73 - Measuring and Testing
Class 74 - Machine Element or Mechanism
Class 75 - Specialized Metallurgical Processes, Compositions for Use Therein,
        Consolidated Metal Powder Compositions, and Loose Metal Particulate
        Mixtures
Class 76 - Metal Tools and Implements, Making
Class 79 - Button Making
Class 81 - Tools
Class 82 - Turning
Class 83 - Cutting
Class 84 - Music
Class 86 - Ammunition and Explosive Charge Making
Class 87 - Textiles: Braiding, Netting, and Lace Making
Class 89 - Ordnance
Class 91 - Motors: Expansible Chamber Type
Class 92 - Expansible Chamber Devices
Class 95 - Gas Separation: Processes
Class 96 - Gas Separation: Apparatus
Class 99 - Foods and Beverages: Apparatus
Class 100 - Presses
Class 101 - Printing
Class 102 - Ammunition and Explosives
Class 104 - Railways
Class 105 - Railway Rolling Stock
Class 106 - Compositions: Coating or Plastic
Class 108 - Horizontally Supported Planar Surfaces
Class 109 - Safes, Bank Protection, or a Related Device
Class 110 - Furnaces
Class 111 - Planting
Class 112 - Sewing
Class 114 - Ships
Class 116 - Signals and Indicators
Class 117 - Single-Crystal, Oriented-Crystal, and Epitaxy Growth
        Processes; Non-Coating Apparatus Therefor
Class 118 - Coating Apparatus
Class 119 - Animal Husbandry
Class 122 - Liquid Heaters and Vaporizers
Class 123 - Internal-Combustion Engines
Class 124 - Mechanical Guns and Projectors
Class 125 - Stone Working
Class 126 - Stoves and Furnaces
Class 127 - Sugar, Starch, and Carbohydrates
Class 128 - Surgery
Class 131 - Tobacco
Class 132 - Toilet
Class 134 - Cleaning and Liquid Contact with Solids
Class 135 - Tent, Canopy, Umbrella, or Cane
Class 136 - Batteries: Thermoelectric and Photoelectric
Class 137 - Fluid Handling
Class 138 - Pipes and Tubular Conduits
Class 139 - Textiles: Weaving
Class 140 - Wireworking

Class 141 - Fluent Material Handling, with Receiver or Receiver Coacting Means
Class 142 - Wood Turning
Class 144 - Woodworking
Class 147 - Coopering
Class 148 - Metal Treatment
Class 149 - Explosive and Thermic Compositions or Charges
Class 150 - Purses, Wallets, and Protective Covers
Class 152 - Resilient Tires and Wheels
Class 156 - Adhesive Bonding and Miscellaneous Chemical Manufacture
Class 157 - Wheelwright Machines
Class 159 - Concentrating Evaporators
Class 160 - Flexible or Portable Closure, Partition, or Panel
Class 162 - Paper Making and Fiber Liberation
Class 163 - Needle and Pin Making
Class 164 - Metal Founding
Class 165 - Heat Exchange
Class 166 - Wells
Class 168 - Farriery
Class 169 - Fire Extinguishers
Class 171 - Unearthing Plants or Buried Objects
Class 172 - Earth Working
Class 173 - Tool Driving or Impacting
Class 174 - Electricity: Conductors and Insulators
Class 175 - Boring or Penetrating the Earth
Class 177 - Weighing Scales
Class 178 - Telegraphy
Class 180 - Motor Vehicles
Class 181 - Acoustics
Class 182 - Fire Escape, Ladder, or Scaffold
Class 184 - Lubrication
Class 185 - Motors: Spring, Weight, or Animal Powered
Class 186 - Merchandising
Class 187 - Elevators
Class 188 - Brakes
Class 190 - Trucks and Hand-Carried Luggage
Class 191 - Electricity: Transmission to Vehicles
Class 192 - Clutches and Power-Stop Control
Class 193 - Conveyors, Chutes, Skids, Guides, and Ways
Class 194 - Check-Actuated Control Mechanisms
Class 196 - Mineral Oils: Apparatus
Class 198 - Conveyors: Power-Driven
Class 199 - Type Casting
Class 200 - Electricity: Circuit Makers and Breakers
Class 201 - Distillation: Processes, Thermolytic
Class 202 - Distillation: Apparatus
Class 203 - Distillation: Processes, Separatory
Class 204 - Chemistry: Electrical and Wave Energy
Class 205 - Electrolysis: Processes, Compositions Used Therein, and
                Methods of Preparing the Compositions
Class 206 - Special Receptacle or Package
Class 208 - Mineral Oils: Processes and Products
Class 209 - Classifying, Separating, and Assorting Solids
Class 210 - Liquid Purification or Separation
Class 211 - Supports: Racks
Class 212 - Traversing Hoists

Class 213 - Railway Draft Appliances
Class 215 - Bottles and Jars
Class 217 - Wooden Receptacles
Class 219 - Electric Heating
Class 220 - Receptacles
Class 221 - Article Dispensing
Class 222 - Dispensing
Class 223 - Apparel Apparatus
Class 224 - Package and Article Carriers
Class 225 - Severing by Tearing or Breaking
Class 226 - Advancing Material of Indeterminate Length
Class 227 - Elongated-Member-Driving Apparatus
Class 228 - Metal Fusion Bonding
Class 229 - Envelopes, Wrappers, and Paperboard Boxes
Class 231 - Whips and Whip Apparatus
Class 232 - Deposit and Collection Receptacles
Class 234 - Selective Cutting (e.g., Punching)
Class 235 - Registers
Class 236 - Automatic Temperature and Humidity Regulation
Class 237 - Heating Systems
Class 238 - Railways: Surface Track
Class 239 - Fluid Sprinkling, Spraying, and Diffusing
Class 241 - Solid Material Comminution or Disintegration
Class 242 - Winding, Tensioning, or Guiding
Class 244 - Aeronautics
Class 245 - Wire Fabrics and Structure
Class 246 - Railway Switches and Signals
Class 248 - Supports
Class 249 - Static Molds
Class 250 - Radiant Energy
Class 251 - Valves and Valve Actuation
Class 252 - Compositions
Class 254 - Implements or Apparatus for Applying Pushing or Pulling Force
Class 256 - Fences
Class 257 - Active Solid-State Devices
Class 258 - Railway Mail Delivery
Class 260 - Chemistry of Carbon Compounds
Class 261 - Gas and Liquid Contact Apparatus
Class 264 - Plastic and Nonmetallic Article Shaping or Treating Processes
Class 266 - Metallurgical Apparatus
Class 267 - Spring Devices
Class 269 - Work Holders
Class 270 - Sheet-Material Associating
Class 271 - Sheet Feeding or Delivering
Class 273 - Amusement Devices: Games
Class 276 - Typesetting
Class 277 - Joint Packing
Class 278 - Land Vehicles: Animal Draft Appliances
Class 279 - Chucks or Sockets
Class 280 - Land Vehicles
Class 281 - Books, Strips, and Leaves
Class 283 - Printed Matter
Class 285 - Pipe Joints or Couplings
Class 289 - Knots and Knot Tying
Class 290 - Prime-Mover Dynamo Plants

Class 291 - Track Sanders
Class 292 - Closure Fasteners
Class 293 - Vehicle Fenders
Class 294 - Handling: Hand and Hoist-Line Implements
Class 295 - Railway Wheels and Axles
Class 296 - Land Vehicles: Bodies and Tops
Class 297 - Chairs and Seats
Class 298 - Land Vehicles: Dumping
Class 299 - Mining or in situ Disintegration of Hard Material
Class 300 - Brush, Broom, and Mop Making
Class 301 - Land Vehicles: Wheels and Axles
Class 303 - Fluid-Pressure Brake and Analogous Systems
Class 305 - Wheel Substitutes for Land Vehicles
Class 307 - Electrical Transmission or Interconnection Systems
Class 310 - Electrical Generator or Motor Structure
Class 312 - Supports: Cabinet Structure
Class 313 - Electric Lamp and Discharge Devices
Class 314 - Electric Lamp and Discharge Devices: Consumable Electrodes
Class 315 - Electric Lamp and Discharge Devices: Systems
Class 318 - Electricity: Motive Power Systems
Class 320 - Electricity: Battery and Condenser Charging and Discharging
Class 322 - Electricity: Single Generator Systems
Class 323 - Electricity: Power Supply or Regulation Systems
Class 324 - Electricity: Measuring and Testing
Class 328 - Miscellaneous Electron Space Discharge Device Systems
Class 329 - Demodulators
Class 330 - Amplifiers
Class 331 - Oscillators
Class 332 - Modulators
Class 333 - Wave Transmission Lines and Networks
Class 334 - Tuners
Class 335 - Electricity: Magnetically Operated Switches, Magnets, and Electromagnets
Class 336 - Inductor Devices
Class 337 - Electricity: Electrothermally or Thermally Actuated Switches
Class 338 - Electrical Resistors
Class 340 - Communications: Electrical
Class 341 - Coded Data Generation or Conversion
Class 342 - Communications: Directive Radio Wave Systems and Devices
          (e.g., Radar, Radio Navigation)
Class 343 - Communications: Radio Wave Antennas
Class 345 - Selective Visual Display Systems
Class 346 - Recorders
Class 347 - Incremental Printing of Symbolic Information
Class 348 - Television
Class 351 - Optics: Eye Examining, Vision Testing and Correcting
Class 352 - Optics: Motion Pictures
Class 353 - Optics: Image Projectors
Class 354 - Photography
Class 355 - Photocopying
Class 356 - Optics: Measuring and Testing
Class 358 - Facsimile or Television Recording
Class 359 - Optics: Systems (Including Communication) and Elements
Class 360 - Dynamic Magnetic Information Storage or Retrieval
Class 361 - Electricity: Electrical Systems and Devices
Class 362 - Illumination

Class 363 - Electric Power Conversion Systems
Class 364 - Electrical Computers and Data Processing Systems
Class 365 - Static Information Storage and Retrieval
Class 366 - Agitating
Class 367 - Communications, Electrical: Acoustic Wave Systems and Devices
Class 368 - Horology: Time Measuring Systems or Devices
Class 369 - Dynamic Information Storage or Retrieval
Class 370 - Multiplex Communications
Class 371 - Error Detection/Correction and Fault Detection/Recovery
Class 372 - Coherent Light Generators
Class 373 - Industrial Electric Heating Furnaces
Class 374 - Thermal Measuring and Testing
Class 375 - Pulse or Digital Communications
Class 376 - Induced Nuclear Reactions: Processes, Systems, and Elements
Class 377 - Electrical Pulse Counters, Pulse Dividers, or Shift Registers:
           Circuits and Systems
Class 378 - X-Ray or Gamma Ray Systems or Devices
Class 379 - Telephonic Communications
Class 380 - Cryptography
Class 381 - Electrical Audio Signal Processing Systems and Devices
Class 382 - Image Analysis
Class 383 - Flexible Bags
Class 384 - Bearings
Class 385 - Optical Waveguides
Class 388 - Electricity: Motor Control Systems
Class 392 - Electric Resistance Heating Devices
Class 395 - Information Processing System Organization
Class 400 - Typewriting Machines
Class 401 - Coating Implements with Material Supply
Class 402 - Binder Device Releasably Engaging Aperture or Notch of Sheet
Class 403 - Joints and Connections
Class 404 - Road Structure, Process, or Apparatus
Class 405 - Hydraulic and Earth Engineering
Class 406 - Conveyors: Fluid Current
Class 407 - Cutters, for Shaping
Class 408 - Cutting by Use of Rotating Axially Moving Tool
Class 409 - Gear Cutting, Milling, or Planing
Class 410 - Freight Accommodation on Freight Carrier
Class 411 - Expanded, Threaded, Driven, Headed, Tool-Deformed, or
           Locked-Threaded Fasteners
Class 412 - Bookbinding: Process and Apparatus
Class 413 - Sheet Metal Container Making
Class 414 - Material or Article Handling
Class 415 - Rotary Kinetic Fluid Motors or Pumps
Class 416 - Fluid Reaction Surfaces (i.e., Impellers)
Class 417 - Pumps
Class 418 - Rotary Expansible Chamber Devices
Class 419 - Powder Metallurgy Processes
Class 420 - Alloys or Metallic Compositions
Class 422 - Chemical Apparatus and Process Disinfecting, Deodorizing,
           Preserving, or Sterilizing
Class 423 - Chemistry of Inorganic Compounds
Class 424 - Drug, Bio-Affecting and Body Treating Compositions
Class 425 - Plastic Article or Earthenware Shaping or Treating
Class 426 - Food or Edible Material: Processes, Compositions, and Products

Class 427 - Coating Processes
Class 428 - Stock Material or Miscellaneous Articles
Class 429 - Chemistry: Electrical Current Producing Apparatus,
          Product, and Process
Class 430 - Radiation Imagery Chemistry: Process, Composition, or
          Product Thereof
Class 431 - Combustion
Class 432 - Heating
Class 433 - Dentistry
Class 434 - Education and Demonstration
Class 435 - Chemistry: Molecular Biology and Microbiology
Class 436 - Chemistry: Analytical and Immunological Testing
Class 437 - Semiconductor Device Manufacturing: Process
Class 439 - Electrical Connectors
Class 440 - Marine Propulsion
Class 441 - Buoys, Rafts, and Aquatic Devices
Class 445 - Electric Lamp or Space Discharge Component or Device Manufacturing
Class 446 - Amusement Devices: Toys
Class 449 - Bee Culture
Class 450 - Foundation Garments
Class 452 - Butchering
Class 453 - Coin Handling
Class 454 - Ventilation
Class 455 - Telecommunications
Class 460 - Crop Threshing or Separating
Class 462 - Books, Strips, and Leaves for Manifolding
Class 464 - Rotary Shafts, Gudgeons, Housings, and Flexible Couplings
          For Rotary Shafts
Class 470 - Headed Fastener, or Washer Making: Process and Apparatus
Class 472 - Amusement Devices
Class 473 - Amusement Devices: Games
Class 474 - Endless Belt Power Transmission Systems or Components
Class 475 - Planetary Gear Transmission Systems or Components
Class 476 - Friction Gear Transmission Systems or Components
Class 477 - Interrelated Power Delivery Controls, Including Engine Control
Class 482 - Exercise Devices
Class 483 - Tool Changing
Class 492 - Roll or Roller
Class 493 - Manufacturing Container or Tube from Paper; or Other
          Manufacturing from a Sheet or Web
Class 494 - Imperforate Bowl: Centrifugal Separators
Class 501 - Compositions: Ceramic
Class 502 - Catalyst, Solid Sorbent, or Support Therefor: Product or
          Process of Making
Class 503 - Record Receiver Having Plural Interactive Leaves or a
          Color Former, Method of Use, or Developer Therefor
Class 504 - Plant Protecting and Regulating Compositions
Class 505 - Superconductor Technology: Apparatus, Material, Process
Class 507 - Compositions or Methods of Preparation or Mere Methods
          Of Using Said Compositions or a Compound: for Earth Boring or
          for Preventing Contaminant Deposits in Petroleum Oil Conduits
Class 512 - Perfume Compositions
Class 514 - Drug, Bio-Affecting and Body-Treating Compositions
Class 518 - Chemistry: Fischer-Tropsch Processes; or Purification or
          Recovery of Products Thereof

Class 520 - Synthetic Resins or Natural Rubbers No- Part of the 520 Series
Class 521 - Synthetic Resins
Class 522 - Synthetic Resins or Natural Rubbers No- Part of the Class 520 Series
Class 523 - Synthetic Resins or Natural Rubbers No- Part of the Class 520 Series
Class 524 - Synthetic Resins or Natural Rubbers No- Part of the Class 520 Series
Class 525 - Synthetic Resins or Natural Rubbers No- Part of the Class 520 Series
Class 526 - Synthetic Resins or Natural Rubbers No- Part of the Class 520 Series
Class 527 - Synthetic Resins or Natural Rubbers No- Part of the Class 520 Series
Class 528 - Synthetic Resins or Natural Rubbers No- Part of the Class 520 Series
Class 530 - Chemistry: Natural Resins or Derivatives; Peptides or
            Proteins; Lignins or Reaction Products Thereof
Class 532 - Organic Compounds No- Part of the Class 532 - 570 Series
Class 534 - Organic Compounds No- Part of the Class 532 - 570 Series
Class 536 - Organic Compounds No- Part of the Class 532 - 570 Series
Class 540 - Organic Compounds No- Part of the Class 532 - 570 Series
Class 544 - Organic Compounds No- Part of the Class 532 - 570 Series
Class 546 - Organic Compounds No- Part of the Class 532 - 570 Series
Class 548 - Organic Compounds No- Part of the Class 532 - 570 Series
Class 549 - Organic Compounds No- Part of the Class 532 - 570 Series
Class 552 - Organic Compounds No- Part of the Class 532 - 570 Series
Class 554 - Organic Compounds No- Part of the Class 532 - 570 Series
Class 556 - Organic Compounds No- Part of the Class 532 - 570 Series
Class 558 - Organic Compounds No- Part of the Class 532 - 570 Series
Class 560 - Organic Compounds No- Part of the Class 532 - 570 Series
Class 562 - Organic Compounds No- Part of the Class 532 - 570 Series
Class 564 - Organic Compounds No- Part of the Class 532 - 570 Series
Class 568 - Organic Compounds No- Part of the Class 532 - 570 Series
Class 570 - Organic Compounds No- Part of the Class 532 - 570 Series
Class 585 - Chemistry of Hydrocarbon Compounds
Class 588 - Hazardous or Toxic Waste Destruction or Containment
Class 600 - Surgery
Class 601 - Surgery: Kinesitherapy
Class 602 - Surgery: Splint, Brace, or Bandage
Class 604 - Surgery
Class 606 - Surgery
Class 607 - Surgery: Light, Thermal, and Electrical Application
Class 623 - Prosthesis (i.e., Artificial Body Members), Parts Thereof, or
            Aids and Accessories Therefor
Class 800 - Multicellular Living Organisms and Unmodified Parts Thereof
Class 901 - Robots
Class 902 - Electronic Funds Transfer
Class 930 - Peptide or Protein Sequence
Class 935 - Genetic Engineering: Recombinant DNA Technology, Hybrid Or
            Fused Cell Technology, and Related Manipulations of Nucleic
            Acids
Class 987 - Organic Compounds Containing a Bi, Sb, as, or P Atom or
            Containing a Metal Atom to 8th Group of the Periodic
            System

Table 8

INTERNATIONAL TRADEMARK CLASSES

Goods

Class 1 (Chemicals)
Class 2 (Paints)
Class 3 (Cosmetics and cleaning preparations)
Class 4 (Lubricants and fuels)
Class 5 (Pharmaceuticals)
Class 6 (Metal goods)
Class 7 (Machinery)
Class 8 (Hand tools)
Class 9 (Electrical and scientific apparatus)
Class 10 (Medical apparatus)
Class 11 (Environmental control apparatus)
Class 12 (Vehicles)
Class 13 (Firearms)
Class 14 (Jewelry)
Class 15 (Musical instruments)
Class 16 (Paper goods and printed matter)
Class 17 (Rubber goods)
Class 18 (Leather goods)
Class 19 (Non-metallic building materials)
Class 20 (Furniture and articles not otherwise classified)
Class 21 (Housewares and glass)
Class 22 (Cordage and fibers)
Class 23 (Yarns and threads)
Class 24 (Fabrics)
Class 25 (Clothing)
Class 26 (Fancy goods)
Class 27 (Floor coverings)
Class 28 (Toys and sporting goods)
Class 29 (Meats and processed foods)
Class 30 (Staple foods)

Class 31 (Natural agricultural products)
Class 32 (Light beverages)
Class 33 (Wines and spirits)
Class 34 (Smokers' articles)

Services

Class 35 (Advertising and business services)
Class 36 (Insurance and financial services)
Class 37 (Construction and repair services)
Class 38 (Communication services)
Class 39 (Transportation and storage services)
Class 40 (Material treatment services)
Class 41 (Education and entertainment services)
Class 42 (Miscellaneous services)

Recent Changes in the Classification of Goods and Services

On January 1, 1997, the seventh edition of the Nice Agreement went into effect. As a result of that agreement, changes have been made in U.S. trademark classification policy. Some of the most significant and frequently encountered changes include:

➢ Retail store services (and other retail/distributorship, etc. services) transferred from Class 42 to Class 34.
➢ Computer game programs transferred from Class 28 to Class 9.
➢ Cleaning machines, such as vacuum cleaners and floor polishing machines, transferred from Class 9 to Class 7 with other cleaning machines.
➢ Gas-powered welding apparatus transferred from Class 8 to Class 7.
➢ Lottery services transferred from Class 36 to Class 41.
➢ Videotape editing and other film editing services transferred from Class 40 to Class 41.
➢ Destruction and incineration of waste and trash transferred from Class 42 to Class 40.
➢ Computer programs downloadable from a global computer network transferred from Class 42 to Class 9.

Table 9

SAMPLES OF ONLINE
INTELLECTUAL PROPERTY
SEARCHES

The following materials were prepared for the users of the DIALOG®
online service. The pages are reproduced with permission from Knight-
Ridder Information, Inc.[1]

GENERAL INFORMATION ON SEARCH SOLUTIONS

- Please note that the Search Strategy and associated explanation
  appear in tabular format with the command (when they appear) on
  the left side in **bold** and discussion on the right side. Additional
  information on a command appears by itself (see example below).

?b 226	BEGIN File 226.

Other information related to the above commands and information will appear underneath like this.

- Some long commands wrap in this display (see example below). In
  a real situation, the command should be written on one line without
  any line breaks or returns.

? S S1 or S2	In this example, the command on the left breaks. In a real search, the command would be written on one line with no breaks.

PATENTS

Comprehensive Patent Assignee Searching, Using Patent Assignee Codes

Patent assignee codes are offered in the Derwent World Patents Index (351) and the CLAIMS® (340,341) databases. In addition, the PATFULL records are updated with the CLAIMS® assignee codes. The database producers differ in their criteria for assigning codes. It is important to understand these differences, strengths, and shortcomings in order to use effectively the codes in your search query.

HOW PATENT ASSIGNEE CODES ARE ASSIGNED

CLAIMS (FILES 340,23,24,25,125,341,223,224,225)

The CLAIMS assignee codes are given to companies with chemical patents and to companies (Master Companies) that have 10 or more patents issued in any one calendar year. Currently, there are approximately 27,500 Master Companies. When chemical assignee codes were first given, there were fewer chemical patents and chemical companies. As a result, the codes gave a relatively comprehensive search. Now, between 140-170 new chemical company names are added every month, and this has caused the chemical assignee codes to become less reliable. In contrast, all patents (mechanical, electrical, and chemical) issuing to a Master Company are closely monitored for name variations in spellings, punctuation, abbreviations, and inversions. The integrity of the assignee codes are maintained across changes in the Master Company's name. While divisions of a Master Company are given the same code, subsidiaries are not. In addition, foreign counterparts are assigned different codes.

DERWENT (FILE 351)

Derwent World Patents Index gives a standard four-letter assignee code to approximately 21,000 companies worldwide that have 50 patents or more. These codes retrieve the worldwide holding of a company, as well as its subsidiaries and related companies. Smaller companies are assigned non-standard assignee codes that are shared by companies of similar names. The non-standard codes are distinguished from the standard by punctuation, i.e., hyphen (-) for non-standards, equal (=) for Soviet inventions, or slash (/) for individuals. The codes are not updated to reflect mergers, takeovers, or name changes.

WHEN WOULD ONE SEARCH USING THE CODES?

For a comprehensive patent assignee search in the CLAIMS files, it is recommended that you search the codes and the company name in the PA= field. The preferred approach is:

1. EXPAND the company name in the PA= field.

2. SELECT the E number(s) that correspond to the name.

3. TYPE the first one or two records to check for relevance. Enter PA in the format field, e.g., TYPE S1/PA/1-2. Make a note of the patent assignee code (if present).

4. SELECT the code using the PA= prefix.

5. SELECT the resulting set and OR it with the set obtained from searching the company name in step 2.

Derwent assigns four-letter codes to patent assignees. When performing a search using these four-letter codes in Derwent World Patents Index, your search results may include irrelevant records for companies that contain the four-letter codes as part of the company name. To avoid this, use the Full Filed (/FF) limit suffix to retrieve records that contain those four letters in the Patent Assignee Code field.

Command Summary

B	125,340
E	PA=HOFFMAN LA ROCHE
S	E#
T	S1/PA/1-2
S	PA=CODE
S	S1 OR S2
B	351
E	PA=HOFFMAN LA ROCHE
S	E#
T	S1/PA/1-2
S	CODE/FF
S	S1 OR S2

Search Strategy

TOPIC: How would one search CLAIMS® database, File 340 and Derwent's World Patents Index, File 351, for all patents assigned to Hoffmann La Roche?

?b 125, 340	BEGIN FileS 125, 340. Note that the file banners indicate the last time the file was updated.

```
SYSTEM:OS   - DIALOG OneSearch
   File 125:CLAIMS(R)/US Patent Mar 1996/Jun 11
(c) 1996 IFI/Plenum Data Corp
   File 340:CLAIMS(R)/US PATENTS ABS  1950-
1996/Mar
         (c) 1996 IFI/Plenum Data Corp.

         Set  Items  Description
         ---  -----  -----------
```

? e pa=hoffmann la roche	EXPAND on the company name (patent assignee).

```
Ref    Items   Index-term
E1         9   PA=HOFFMANN L
E2         1   PA=HOFFMANN L A
E3         8  *PA=HOFFMANN LA ROCHE
E4         1   PA=HOFFMANN LA ROCHE &
E5         3   PA=HOFFMANN LA ROCHE & CIE SA F
E6         6   PA=HOFFMANN LA ROCHE & CO AG
E7       659   PA=HOFFMANN LA ROCHE & CO AG F
E8         1   PA=HOFFMANN LA ROCHE & CO KG F
E9         7   PA=HOFFMANN LA ROCHE AG
E10        8   PA=HOFFMANN LA ROCHE AG F
E11        2   PA=HOFFMANN LA ROCHE CO LTD F
E12        2   PA=HOFFMANN LA ROCHE F

         Enter P or PAGE for more
```

? s e8	SELECT appropriate E number.

```
S1    4099  PA="HOFFMANN-LA ROCHE INC"
```

?t 1/pa/1-2	TYPE the first two records using PA in the format field.

```
 1/PA/1      (Item 1 from file: 125)
DIALOG(R)File 125:(c) 1996 IFI/Plenum Data Corp. All
rts. reserv.

Assignee: Hoffmann-La Roche Inc   Assignee Code: 39424

 1/PA/2      (Item 2 from file: 125)
DIALOG(R)File 125:(c) 1996 IFI/Plenum Data Corp. All
rts. reserv.

Assignee: Hoffmann-La Roche Inc   Assignee Code: 39424
```

?s pa=39424	SELECT the PA= code.

```
     S2    4099  PA=39424
```

?s s1 or s2	OR the company set (S1) with the code set (S2).

```
          4099  S1
          4099  S2
     S3   4099  S1 OR S2
```

?b 351	BEGIN File 351.

```
   File 351:DERWENT WPI  1981-
1996/UD=9623;UA=9619;UM=9611
      (c)1996 Derwent Info Ltd

   Set  Items  Description
   ---  -----  -----------
```

?e pa=hoffmann la roche	EXPAND the company name (patent assignee).

```
Ref     Items    Index-term
E1          9     PA=HOFFMANN L
E2          1     PA=HOFFMANN L A
E3          8   * PA=HOFFMANN LA ROCHE
E4          1     PA=HOFFMANN LA ROCHE &
E5          3     PA=HOFFMANN LA ROCHE & CIE SA F
E6          6     PA=HOFFMANN LA ROCHE & CO AG
E7        659     PA=HOFFMANN LA ROCHE & CO AG F
E8          1     PA=HOFFMANN LA ROCHE & CO KG F
E9          7     PA=HOFFMANN LA ROCHE AG
E10         8     PA=HOFFMANN LA ROCHE AG F
E11         2     PA=HOFFMANN LA ROCHE CO LTD F
E12         2     PA=HOFFMANN LA ROCHE F

          Enter P or PAGE for more
```

?s e7	SELECT the appropriate E number.

```
        S1      659   PA="HOFFMANN LA ROCHE & CO AG F"
```

?t 1/pa/1-2	TYPE the first two records using PA in the format field. Note the PA code "HOFF."

```
 1/PA/1
DIALOG(R)File 351:(c)1996 Derwent Info Ltd. All
rts. reserv.

Patent Assignee: HOFF ) HOFFMANN LA ROCHE & CO
AG F

 1/PA/2
DIALOG(R)File 351:(c)1996 Derwent Info Ltd. All
rts. reserv.

Patent Assignee: HOFF ) HOFFMANN LA ROCHE & CO
AG F
```

| ?s pa=hoff/ff | SELECT the PA code and limit retrieval to Full Field (/FF). |

```
    S2      1520   PA=HOFF/FF
```

| ?s s1 or s2 | OR the company set (S1) with code set (S2). |

```
           659  S1
          1520  S2
   S3     1520  S1 OR S2
```

Other Helpful Materials

Other Search Aids	
Online on DIALOG	
DIALOG Bluesheets™, File 415	
ASAF – Call 800-496-4470 or 415-254-8246 to place an order for the following FREE documents:	
Document	**ASAF #**
340 Bluesheet	3340
351 Bluesheet	3351
Smart Tools for Intellectual Property: The Fine Print.	4832
WWW SITES	
www.dialog.com	
DB. PRODUCER:	
IFI/PLENUM for more information on the CLAIMS® files: 800-331-4955	
DERWENT for more information on Derwent World Patents Index: 800-451-3451	

PATENTS

Searching for Atypical U.S. Patent Numbers

There are several types of U.S. patent numbers that do not conform to the standard of a seven-digit number beginning with 3, 4, or 5. Such patent numbers are valid, and can be searched in a variety of databases on DIALOG. Following are examples for Design Patents, Plant Patents, Statutory Invention Registrations, Defensive Publications, Reissue Patents, and U.S. Government Published Patent Applications (NTIS listings).

DESIGN PATENTS

*Where To Search	*DIALOG Format	*Search Example	*How To Search
*CLAIMS® (125,340,341)	*PN=CC DNNNNNN	*S PN=US D253796	*Enter the U.S. country code, a space, and the letter D, followed by a six-digit number.
*U.S. Patents Fulltext (652-654)	*DT=DESIGN	*S DT=DESIGN	*To get all the patents designated as DESIGN, SELECT DT=DESIGN.

PLANT PATENTS

*Where To Search	*DIALOG Format	*Search Example	*How To Search
*CLAIMS (125,340,341) U.S. Patents Fulltext (652-654)	*PN=CC PPNNNNN	*S PN=US PP03996	*Enter the U.S. country code, a space, the letters PP, followed by a five-digit number (fill with leading zeros if needed).

*Where To Search	*DIALOG Format	*Search Example	*How To Search
*INPADOC/ Family and Legal Status (345)	*PN=CC NNNN	*S PN=US 3996	*Enter the U.S. country code, a space, followed by a four-digit number.
*	*PC=CC P	*S PN=US 3996	*To find all the plant patents, enter the U.S. country code, followed by the letter P.

STATUTORY INVENTION REGISTRATIONS

*Where To Search	*DIALOG Format	*Search Example	*How To Search
*CLAIMS (125,340,341) U.S. Patents Fulltext (652-654) DWPI (351)	*PN=CC HNNNN	*S PN=US H1005	*Enter the U.S. country code, a space, and the letter H, followed by a one-to- four-digit number with no leading zeros.
*CLAIMS (125,340,341) U.S. Patents Fulltext (652-654)	*DT= STATUTORY	*S DT= STATUTORY	*To find all the statutory invention disclosures, enter DT= STATUTORY.
*	*PN=CC NNNN	*S PN=US 1005	*Enter the U.S. country code, a space, followed by a four-digit number.
*INPADOC/ Family and Legal Status (345)	*PC=CC H1	*S PN=US H1	*To find all the statutory invention disclosures, enter the U.S. country code, followed by the

			letter H, and a 1.

DEFENSIVE PUBLICATIONS

*Where To Search	*DIALOG Format	*Search Example	*How To Search
*U.S. Patents Fulltext (652-654) CLAIMS (125,340,341) DWPI (351)	*PN=CC TNNNNNN	*S PN=US T101103	*Enter the U.S. country code, a space, and the letter T, followed by a six-digit number.
*CLAIMS (125,340,341)	*DT= DEFENSIVE	*S DT= DEFENSIVE	*To find all the defensive publications, enter DT= DEFENSIVE
*INPADOC/ Family and Legal Status (345) DWPI (351)	*PN=CC NNNNNN	*S PN=US 101103	*Enter the U.S. country code, a space, followed by a six-digit number.
*	*PC=US H	*S PC=US H	*To find all the defensive publications, enter the U.S. country code, followed by the letter H.

REISSUE PATENTS

*Where To Search	*DIALOG Format	*Search Example	*How To Search
*U.S. Patents Fulltext (652-654) CLAIMS (125,340,341) INPADOC/Family and Legal Status (345) DWPI (351)	*PN=CC RENNNNN	*S PN=US RE31794	*Enter the U.S. country code, a space, and the letters RE, followed by a five-digit number.

U.S. GOVERNMENT PUBLISHED PATENT APPLICATIONS (NTIS LISTINGS)

*Where To Search	*DIALOG Format	*Search Example	*How To Search
*DWPI (351) CA SEARCH®: Chemical Abstracts® (399)	*PN=CC 6NNNNNN	*S PN=US 6244571	*Enter the U.S. country code, a space, and the application series number (6,7, or 8), followed by a six-digit number with leading zeros.
*NTIS (6)	*RN= PAT-APPL-7- NNN NNN	*S RN= PAT-APPL-6- 624 564	*The last 6 digits of the patent number usually has a space between the third and fourth number. If you get zero results, try entering the last 6 digits without a space. For Example: S RN=APT- APPL-6- 624564.

Other Helpful Materials

Other Search Aids
Online on DIALOG – (nnn represents the file number)
HELP FMT nnn (for pre-defined format options)
HELP RATES nnn
ASAF – Call 800-496-4470 or 415-254-8246 to place an order for the following FREE documents:

Directory of ASAF Documentation	4000

WWW SITES
www.dialog.com
DB. PRODUCER –
Call 800-451-3451 for more information about Derwent World Patents Index.
Call 800-331-4955 for more information about IFI/Plenum Data Corporation's CLAIMS files.

TRADEMARK INFORMATION

Finding U.S. Trademarks

When searching in the TRADEMARKSCAN® files, there are three ways to find a trademark that mentions a particular word:

- searching for the word or prefix
- searching for an exact match of the word or prefix

Searching in the Rotated Trademark (TR=) field provides the broadest possible retrieval. When searching in the TR= field, the DIALOG system looks for the occurrence of the specified string of letters anywhere in the record, including when the letters in the string appear as more than one word, when they are separated by punctuation, or when the string has a prefix or suffix, or both. The following examples do not provide a specific search strategy. Instead, they outline the differences between various techniques for trademark word searching. Each of the three techniques provides unique strengths and weaknesses, which are described below.

NOTE: When searching for common character strings, you may receive a message indicating that the DIALOG system has reached the processing limit and has stopped the search. See page 4 for information about continuing the search beyond the processing limit.

Command Summary

B	226,246
S	KID
S	KID?
S	KID? ?
S	K?D

E	ET=KID
S	TR=KID?
S	TR=KID@?
STR	STR=KID@S?

Search Strategy

?b 226,246	BEGIN File 226, TRADEMARKSCAN®-U.S. FEDERAL and File 246-TRADEMARKSCAN®-U.S.-STATE. The search will be processed simultaneously in two databases.
? s kid	This method searches the word "kid" as a whole word, with no plurals, prefixes, suffixes, or alternate spellings. It retrieves any trademark with the word "kid" in it. This method is the simplest possible search.

S1   5065   KID

? s kid?	This method searches the word "kid" as a whole word or prefix. Words like "kidding," "kids," or "kidder" will be retrieved. This method is a broad search.

S2   5686   KID?

?s kid? ?	This method searches the word "kid" as a whole word with a single additional letter. The word "kids" will be retrieved, but not the word "kidding."

```
S3     5119  KID?  ?
```

?s k?d	This method searches for any individual character between the letters "k" and "d." Words like "kid" or "kad" will be retrieved. This method is very helpful if there is a question about the correct spelling of a word.

```
        S4     5149   K?D
```

?e et=kid	This method searches for the word "kid" as an exact trademark. By EXPANDing on the term in the Exact Trademark (ET=) field, a list of everything alphabetically close to the desired word is displayed. To retrieve the term of choice, select the E number. Multiple E numbers can be selected at the same time.

```
Ref    Items   Index-term

E1       1    ET=KICKY NICKY
E2       1    ET=KICO-COOLER
E3       4   *ET=KID
E4       1    ET=KID 'N' ME
E5       1    ET=KID ALERT LATCHKEY KID
E6       1    ET=KID AMERICA
E7       2    ET=KID ANGELS
E8       2    ET=KID APPEAL
E9       1    ET=KID APPROVED
E10      1    ET=KID ARMOR
E11      1    ET=KID ASHWORTH
E12      2    ET=KID ATHLETE
        Enter P or PAGE for more
```

```
?s e3
```

```
S5          4   ET="KID"
```

?s tr=kid?	This method searches for the word "kid" as a whole word, prefix, suffix, and mid-word string. Words like "kid," "kids," or "skidaddle" will be retrieved. This method will also retrieve the string of letters "kid" with any combination of spaces or punctuation marks, like "quick-id." This search will NOT work without a question mark. This method is the broadest search possible.

```
S6      6099   TR=KID?
```

?s tr=kid@?	This method searches the word "kid" as a whole word or suffix in the trademark. Words like "adikid" will be retrieved.

```
S7      1462   TR=KID@?
```

?s tr=kid@s?	This method retrieves any word in a trademark phrase that starts with an "s" and ends with "kid." Words like "snowkid" or "smartkid" will be retrieved.

```
S8       72   TR=KID@S?
```

Occasionally searching for a trademark with a short character string produces a processing limit message. When searching for tr=me?, the DIALOG system cannot process all of the different options and a processing limit message appears, displaying at what point DIALOG stopped searching for the term.

?s tr=me?	This is an example of the processing limit message when the system cannot process all of the different options of a search term.

```
>>>File 226 processing for TR=ME? stopped at TR=MER@SUPERPR
     S1    79607   TR=ME?
```

?s tr=mer@super pr : tr=me9999	To continue the search, enter a statement that includes the last term searched (as shown in the processing limit message) and ends with "9999."

```
     S2    48220   TR=MER@SUPERPR : TR=ME9999
```

?s s1 or s2	OR the sets together to have one complete set of all the possible options.

```
          79607   S1
          48220   S2
     S3  123943   S1 OR S2
```

A final note when searching for words in a trademark. Thomson & Thomson cross-references variant spellings within the database. When a word is spelled in an unusual way, such as "klassix" instead of "classics," search for the correct spelling. The correct spelling will retrieve the variation.

Other Helpful Materials

Other Search Aids	
DIALOG TRADEMARKSCAN Databases	
North American TRADEMARKSCAN Files:	
U.S. FEDERAL (File 226)	U.S. STATE (File 246)
CANADA (File 127)	
European and International Trademarks:	
AUSTRIA (File 662)	ITALY (File 673)
BENELUX (File 658)	LIECHTENSTEIN (File 677)
DENMARK (File 659)	MONACO (File 663)
FRANCE (File 657)	SWITZERLAND (File 661)
GERMANY (File 672)	U.K. (File 126)
INTERNATIONAL REGISTER (File 671)	
OneSearch® Categories:	
TRADEMKS, TMKS (all TRADEMARKSCAN files)	
EUROTMKS (all European and INTERNATIONAL REGISTER files)	
NATMKS (all North American TRADEMARKSCAN files)	
WWW SITES	
www.dialog.com	
http://www.thomson-thomson.com	
DB. PRODUCER:	
Thomson & Thomson also provides a customer service help desk and training: 800-692-8833	

TRADEMARK DATABASES

Locating Common Law Uses of Trademarks

The application and subsequent registration of a unique trademark on federal, state, or international levels provides maximum protection, but it is important to recognize that "Common Law" or unregistered trademarks are also legally protected. The TRADEMARKSCAN ®- U.S. FEDERAL, STATE, and international files are the best places to conduct the preliminary screening and to ensure ongoing protection of pending and registered trademarks. After a preliminary search, the following strategy will help to ascertain whether a mark is being used in commerce during both preliminary screening and for ongoing protection and maintenance of a trademark.

Command Summary

B	TMKS
S	S TR=WORD? and TR=WORD?
B	116
Search as TN= or TR=(in the rotated index) for the trade name	
B	416
E	Expand CO= (company name)
B	PAPERSMJ or PAPERS
Search uncommon terms in free text	
B	411
Set Files(SF)to appropriate DIALINDEX® category depending on the industry or proposed use of mark	

Search Strategy

?b tmks	BEGIN TMKS to search in all trademark files.
? ss tr=mocha? and tr=marvel?	Use TR= with truncation to retrieve marks with "mocha" and "marvel" as a prefix, suffix, or mid-word string.

```
S1      207   TR=MOCHA?
S2      829   TR=MARVEL?
S3        0   TR=MOCHA? AND TR=MARVEL?
```

? s s2 and ic=30	Combine with the international class code for staple foods.

```
         829   S2
      593291   IC=30
S4        68   S2 AND IC=30
```

?s s4/active	Limit to active applications or registrations.

```
S5        56   S4/ACTIVE
```

? t s5/49/all	TYPE your set in Format 49 to display just the text of the mark.

```
5/49/1      (Item 1 from file: 226)
04603004
MARVELOAF

 5/49/2      (Item 2 from file: 226)
04038861
MARAVILLAS
          (...)
```

? b 116	BEGIN File 116.

```
File 116:Brands & their Companies 1995/Feb
       (c) 1995 Gale Research Inc
```

? ss tr=mocha? and tr=marvel?	Use the rotated trademark index, TR=, for the broadest search.

```
        S1      17   TR=MOCHA?
        S2      99   TR=MARVEL?
        S3       0   TR=MOCHA? AND TR=MARVEL?
```

? s s2 and ic=(30 or 42)	Refine the search by "AND"ing search terms with the industry codes (IC) that correspond to International Class Codes used in the TRADEMARKSCAN files.

```
        99   S2
     20104   IC=30
       790   IC=42
  S4     4   S2 AND IC=(30 OR 42)
```

```
? t s4/3/1-5
```

```
DIALOG(R)File 116:Brands & their Companies
(c) 1995 Gale Research Inc. All rts. reserv.

09969065
 SUBFILE: Brands and Their Companies
 TRADE NAME:  MINT MARVELS
 DESCRIPTION: Candy novelties

 4/3/2
DIALOG(R)File 116:Brands & their Companies
(c) 1995 Gale Research Inc. All rts. reserv.

09912391
 SUBFILE: Brands and Their Companies
 TRADE NAME:  MARVEL
 DESCRIPTION: Yeast, now out of production

 4/3/3
DIALOG(R)File 116:Brands & their Companies
(c) 1995 Gale Research Inc. All rts. reserv.
```

```
09900627
 SUBFILE: Brands and Their Companies
 TRADE NAME:  MARVEL
 DESCRIPTION: Bread

 4/3/4
DIALOG(R)File 116:Brands & their Companies
(c) 1995 Gale Research Inc. All rts. reserv.

09808165
 SUBFILE: Brands and Their Companies
 TRADE NAME:  MARVELOUS CREATIONS
 DESCRIPTION: Baking mixes
```

? **b 416**	BEGIN File 416 . This file allows quick identification of files that have information on a particular company.

```
File 416:DIALOG COMPANY NAME FINDER(TM)
1996/MAR
        (c) 1996 Dialog Info.Svcs.

   Set   Items  Description
   ---   -----  -----------
```

? **e co=mocha mar**	When the exact name is unknown, the CO= index may be EXPANDed to browse company name variations. Most DIALOG databases that index a company name in the Additional Indexes are included in the database.

```
Ref     Items   Index-term
E1        1     CO=MOCHA MANSION INC THE
E2        1     CO=MOCHA MANUFACTURING COMPANY LIMITED
E3        0    *CO=MOCHA MAR
E4        3     CO=MOCHA MARKETPLACE
E5        2     CO=MOCHA MEN WEST
E6        3     CO=MOCHA MIST BEAUTY SALON
E7        1     CO=MOCHA MOCHA
E8        1     CO=MOCHA MOCHA CAFE
E9        1     CO=MOCHA MODEMS
E10       1     CO=MOCHA MOLLY S
E11       2     CO=MOCHA MOLLYS COF SLON
E12       1     CO=MOCHA MOSQUE
                Enter P or PAGE for more
```

? s mocha? and marvel?	

```
          461   MOCHA?
         2859   MARVEL?
   S1        0  MOCHA? AND MARVEL?
```

? b papersmj	BEGIN PAPERSMJ to search the free text of major newspapers.
? s mocha?(2n)marvel?	

```
         3141   MOCHA?
        93221   MARVEL?
   S1        3  MOCHA?(2N)MARVEL?
```

? t s1/6,k/all	TYPE records in Format 6,K to display titles and the "Key Words In Context" to determine if the phrase is a common usage phrase or a possible common law use of the phrase. For format pricing, enter HELP RATES 146.

```
 1/6,K/1      (Item 1 from file: 146)
DIALOG(R)File 146:(c) 1996 Washington Post. All
rts. reserv.

2020644
DINING -Leesburg's Cultivated Cooking.
Line Count: 94     Word Count: 1038

... exceptional house-made sorbets, aromatic
with fresh fruit; a devil's food cake oozing a
marvelous mocha cream; an elegant lemon
poundcake
fragrant with fresh lemon sauce; an exquisite
pecan toffee torte...

 1/6,K/2      (Item 1 from file: 630)
DIALOG(R)File 630:(c) 1996 Los Angeles Times.
All rts. reserv.

02238611                    00395
ALL THAT SIZZLES
Deep-Fried Catfish, Chinese Ravioli, Shiitake
Salad: Just Three Reasons Why Shiro Shines
Word Count: 891

Los Angeles Times_1985-1996/Maicy 01
TEXT:
     ...mousse tart. A dark, tender chocolate
mousse cake comes with vanilla ice cream and a
marvelous mocha sauce. But for me, the ideal
ending to a Shiro meal is his deep- fried...
     (...)
```

? **b 411**	BEGIN 411. DIALINDEX® identifies databases containing information on a given subject.

```
File 411:DIALINDEX(R)
DIALINDEX(R)
   (c) 1996 Knight-Ridder Info
```

*** DIALINDEX search results display in an abbreviated
*** format unless you enter the SET DETAIL ON command.

? **sf products,** **tradenms**	Specify the files to be searched with the SET FILES command.

You have 40 files in your file list.
(To see banners, use SHOW FILES command)

?s **mocha?(2n)marvel?**

```
Your SELECT statement is:
 s mocha?(2n)marvel?
 Items File
 ----- ----
 2     9: Business & Industry(TM)_Jul 1994-1996/May 03
 1    16: IAC PROMT(R)_1972-1996/May 03
 1   636: IAC Newsletter DB(TM)_1987-1996/May 03
 1   570: IAC MARS(R)_1984-1996/May 03
```

4 files have one or more items; file list includes 40
files.

? **rank files**	Rank results in order by the number of items retrieved from each file by entering the RANK FILES (RF) command.

```
Your last SELECT statement was:
  S MOCHA?(2N)MARVEL?

Ref    Items    File
---    -----    ----
N1     2         9: Business & Industry(TM)_Jul 1994-
1996/May 03
N2     1        16: IAC PROMT(R)_1972-1996/May 03
N3     1       636: IAC Newsletter DB(TM)_1987-1996/May 03
N4     1       570: IAC MARS(R)_1984-1996/May 03
N5     0        47: Magazine Database(TM)_1959-1996/May 03
N6     0        80: IAC Aerospace/Def.Mkts(R)_1986-1996/May
03
N7     0       111: Natl.Newspaper Index(TM)_1979-1996/Mar
N8     0       116: Brands & their Companies_1995/Feb
N9     0       148: IAC Trade & Industry Database_1976-
1996/May 03
N10    0       149: IAC(SM) Health & Wellness DB(SM)_76-
96/Apr W5
    4 files have one or more items; file list includes
40 files.

        - Enter P or PAGE for more -

N numbers can be used to begin a search in the desired
files.
```

? **save temp**	Use SAVE TEMP to save the search and re-execute it in the DIALOG files with results.

```
Temp SearchSave "TD314" stored
```

? **b n1:n4**	Begin N number(s) of files in which you want to search.

```
SYSTEM:OS  - DIALOG OneSearch
  File    9:Business & Industry(TM)   Jul 1994-1996/May
03
         (c) 1996 Resp. DB Svcs.
  File   16:IAC PROMT(R)   1972-1996/May 03
         (c) 1996 Information Access Co.
  File 636:IAC Newsletter DB(TM)   1987-1996/May 03
         (c) 1996 Information Access Co.
 File 570:IAC MARS(R)   1984-1996/May 03
         (c) 1996 Information Access Co.

       Set   Items   Description
       ---   -----   -----------
```

? **exs**	EXECUTE your SearchSave from DIALINDEX® to automatically retrieve the records with hits.

```
Executing TD314
>>>SET HILIGHT: use ON, OFF, or 1-5 characters
              1973   MOCHA?
              6011   MARVEL?
         S1      5   MOCHA?(2N)MARVEL?
```

?rd	Use the RD comand to remove duplicates.

```
         S2      2   RD (unique items)
```

?t s1/3,k/all	TYPE records in Format 3,K to retrieve the bibliographic citations with the descriptors and "key words in context."

```
 2/3,K/1      (Item 1 from file: 9)
DIALOG(R)File    9:Business & Industry(TM)
(c) 1996 Resp. DB Svcs. All rts. reserv.

01373373
Sassy Sol Food Biscookies - Wildest Chocolate Fantasy;
 Mocha Mountain Marvel; Real Grande Chocolate; Orange
Pistachio Rage; Sassy Molasses Spice; Lemon S'Ole
(Sassy Sol Food Biscookies launched by Sassy Sol Food
div of The Real Grande Gorge Cookie Co of New Mexico)
Product Alert, v 25, n 49, p N/A
December 04, 1995
DOCUMENT TYPE: Journal
LANGUAGE: English  RECORD TYPE: Fulltext
WORD COUNT:   91

Sassy Sol Food Biscookies - Wildest Chocolate Fantasy;
 Mocha Mountain  Marvel; Real Grande Chocolate; Orange
Pistachio Rage; Sassy Molasses Spice; Lemon S'Ole


TEXT:
...in 1.5 oz. boxes, as well as in 10 oz. boxes.
Wildest Chocolate Fantasy, Mocha  Mountain Marvel ,
Real Grande Chocolate, Orange Pistachio Rage, Sassy
Molasses Spice and Lemon S'Ole varieties are...

 2/3,K/2      (Item 2 from file: 9)
DIALOG(R)File    9:Business & Industry(TM)
(c) 1996 Resp. DB Svcs. All rts. reserv.

01277680
Sassy Sol Food Biscookies
(Sassy Sol Food introduces Sassy Sol Food Biscookies
in eight varieties)
Snack Food, v 84, n 9, p 17
September 1995
DOCUMENT TYPE: Journal  ISSN: 0037-7406
LANGUAGE: English  RECORD TYPE: Fulltext
WORD COUNT:   111


TEXT:
...flavors and color, Topping contains turbinado sugar

Vital Statistics: Real Grande Chocolate, Wildest
Chocolate Fantasy, Mocha Mountain Marvel , Lemon
S'Ole, Sassy Molasses Spice and Orange Pistachio Rage
varieties.  A portion of the...
```

Other Helpful Materials

Related Files
DIALOG
Recommended OneSearch®/DIALINDEX® Categories include:
• PRODUCTS
• TRADENMS
• NEWSCO
For unique trademarks use the DIALINDEX ALL category.
Other Search Aids
Online on DIALOG – (nnn represents the file number)
HELP FIELDS NNN
HELP FORMATS NNN
HELP RATES NNN
DIALOG Bluesheets®, File 415
ASAF – Call 800-496-4470 or 415-254-8246 to place an order for the following FREE documents:

Document	ASAF #
DIALINDEX Bluesheet	3411
Brands and their Cos. Bluesheet	3116

WWW SITES
www.dialog.com
http://thomson-thomson.com/
DB PRODUCER:
Call Thomson & Thomson at 800-692-8833 to order TRADEMARKSCAN on DIALOG Quick Reference Card.

U.S. COPYRIGHTS

Searching for U.S. Copyright Titles

File 120, **U.S. Copyrights,** provides access to registration details for all active copyright and mask work registrations on file at the U.S. Copyright Office.

This document includes:

- A search example for a given copyright title.
- Answers to frequently asked questions on copyrights, as well as search features.

SEARCHING FOR A COPYRIGHT TITLE

Let's assume that you were given the title "It's Time for a Change," and were informed that this was a musical work, and you had one of the names of the authors listed on the physical work deposited and/or listed on the application for copyright – Robert Kane. A recommended strategy for retrieving this record would be as follows.

Command Summary

B	120
S	ITS TIME FOR A CHANGE?/TF,NF
S	S1 AND RC=M
ST	S2 AND AU=KANE, ROGER?
T	S3/9/1

Search Strategy

?b 120	BEGIN File120.
? s its time for a change?/tf,nf	SELECT the title phrase in the Title of the Registered Work (/TF) field and in the Named Titles (/NF) field.

S1   27   ITS TIME FOR A CHANGE?/TF,NF

? s s1 and rc=m	Combine the previous set with the Library of Congress Retrieval Code for Musical Works.

```
         27    S1
    2637924    RC=M   (MUSICAL WORKS)
S2        18    S1 AND RC=M
```

? s s2 and ua=kane, roger?	Combine the set with the name of an author listed on the physical work and/or listed on the application for copyright.

```
        18    S2
         7    AU=KANE, ROGER?
S3        1    S2 AND AU=KANE, ROGER?
```

?t 3/9/1	TYPE out the record in full record format.

```
3/9/1

DIALOG(R)File 120:US Copyrights

(c) format only 1996 Dialog Info.Svcs. All rts.
reserv.

        01591239

It's time for a change : or, How to entertain yourself
on election day / [by Roger Kane ; cover ill. and
cartoons by Carl Kragelund].

        CLASS:  PA (Performing Arts)
        LC RETRIEVAL CODE: M   (Musical Works)
        STATUS: Registered
        REGISTRATION NUMBER: PA86005
        DATE REGISTERED: September 11, 1980
(19800911)
        PREVIOUS REGISTRATION/PUBLICATION: 2 songs
prev. reg. in Here goes everything, volume I, no. 215-
570.
        DATE OF CREATION: 1980
```

```
              DATE OF PUBLICATION: August 22, 1980
              AUTHOR(s): Kragelund, Carl; Kane, Roger,
1927-
              OWNER(s) : Kane, Roger, 1927-
              LIMITATION OR NEW MATTER: NM: new limericks
& verses.
              NOTES: Collection of song lyrics & verse.
              IMPRINT: Spokane : Kane, [19--]
              REGISTRATION DEPOSIT: 14 p.
              MISCELLANEOUS: C.O. corres.
```

NOTE: If you are not limiting by Library of Congress retrieval codes (RC=), you may retrieve both Monograph Copyright and Legal Document records. You can limit to Monograph Copyright records using the /C suffix, e.g., SELECT S1/C. You can limit to Legal Document records by using the /D suffix, e.g., SELECT S1/D. To avoid displaying an excessively long legal document, use the /2,KWIC format, e.g., TYPE S2/2,KWIC/ALL.

FREQUENTLY ASKED QUESTIONS

Why can't I find this copyright? I know it's still registered.

- The file does not contain all registered works; coverage goes back to around 1964.

- There is a lag time for registrations and often a backlog. The lag time for legal documents can be as long as a year.

- File 120 does NOT include serials, such as periodicals, newsletters, and books that are published annually.

How long before copyrights have to be renewed?

- The Copyrights Act of 1976 changed the duration of copyright registrations; the Act became effective January 1, 1978 and duration dates are based on different factors. Generally speaking:

- For most works since 1978, the term of registration is for the life of the author plus 50 years.

- Prior to 1978, a term of registration was 28 years with the right to renew for another term.

What's a legal document? How is it different from a monograph?

- The legal document is any legal use of the registered work. File 120 contains assignments, licenses, and security interests.

- The monograph is the initial registration of the work.

How can I limit my search by record type?

- SELECT search terms using the /C suffix for monograph or /D for legal. For example, enter S S1/C to create a set composed solely of monograph copyright records.

What format is best for long legal documents?

- Use Format 2 combined with KWIC (Key Word In Context) for a display containing most pertinent data. Remember that KWIC can only work in records no longer than 32,000 words. For pricing information, enter HELP RATES 120.

What's the best way to search a title? What's the difference between Title of Registered Work and Named Titles?

- Unless the search is for legal documents only, it's advisable to search both indexes, /TI,NT to search by individual words or /TF,NF to search by phrase.

- Searching by Title of Registered Work (/TI or /TF) limits retrieval to:

  - The title in the monograph, which also may be the application title or additional titles of renewals.

  - The "Works" section of the legal document (in these records the title listings can be quite long).

- Searching by Named Titles (/NT or /NF) broadens the search to include fields only in the monograph record, such as:

  - Contents – as in the individual songs on a CD sound recording.

  - IN – the title of another work that contains this registered work.

  - Notes – bibliographic comments about the work.

  - Series Statement – the series title where the registered work is part of a set or part of an indefinite sequence of works that have a common title.

  - Contributions – multiple works that are registered as part of a group, e.g., a syndicated news column.

What's the best way to search a one-word title?

- Use the phrase-indexed suffixes /TF, NF, for example, SELECT FEVER/TF,NF.

What's the best way to search a title with punctuation?

- Punctuation is deleted and can be searched

  - as a phrase: SELECT JESSES GIRL/TF,NF or

  - s words: SELECT JESSES(W)GIRL/TI,NT

- Use quotation marks around words in titles containing non-searchable punctuation, e.g,

  - SELECT WHAT THE "*@#?!" IS THAT?/TF,NF

What's the difference between a class and a retrieval code?

- All monograph records are assigned to one of five distinct two-letter classes.

  - **MW Mask Works** – electronic circuitry products (such as semiconductor chips)

  - **PA** Performing Arts – works intended for delivery or performance (i.e., manuscripts, recorded musical compositions; motion pictures)

  - **SR** Sound Recordings – sounds fixed on cassettes, tapes, records, CDs, etc.

  - **TX** Textual Works – non-dramatic textual materials (i.e., pamphlets, microforms, game rules)

  - **VA** Visual Arts – graphic, three-dimensional, or visual fine art (such as technical drawings, photographs)

- Library of Congress retrieval codes categorize the materials deposited.

- Library of Congress retrieval codes:

  - **A Sound Recordings with Non-dramatic Textual Works** (covers both the sound recording and the underlying work).

  - **B Monographic Works of a Non-dramatic Literature Nature**

  - **C Machine-readable Works** (especially computer programs, software, video games, etc.)

- **D Dramatic Works including Accompanying Music** (also includes choreography and pantomimes)
- **E Sound Recordings and Drama** (covers both the sound recording and underlying work)
- **F Cartographic Works** (maps, globes, atlases)
- **M Musical Works**
- **N Sound Records and Music** (covers both the sound recording and underlying work)
- **Q Multimedia and Kit** (two or more distinct media types)
- **S Miscellaneous** (toys, games, small household items, technical drawings and models, jewelry, two-dimensional works of fine and graphic art, commercial prints and labels, photographs and slides, sculptural works, textile fabrics)
- **U Sound Recordings** (only the sound, not the underlying arrangement)
- **X Motion Pictures, Photoplays, Filmstrips** (if the claim is on both the cinematography and music, or on the cinematography and choreography)
- **Z Mask Works** (this is the same as the Class Mask Works)
- **1 Architectural Plans**
- **2 Architectural Plan and Building Design**
- **3 Building Design**
- Some registrations have a third letter "U" which designates the work as "unpublished."

In renewal records, what do the various alpha characters in parentheses represent in the "OWNER(s):" field?

- The Copyright Office uses symbols for the basis of a renewal of the registration. The following symbols are used to indicate who filed for renewal of the copyright.

A	Author(s)
Adm. c.t.a.	Administrator(s) or Administratrix cum testamento annexo

Adm. d.b.n.c.t.a.	Administrator(s) or Administratrix de bonis non cum testamento annexo
C	Child or children of the deceased author
E	Executor(s) or Executrix of the deceased author; includes co-executor, co-executrix, etc.
Successor E	Successor Executor(s) or Executrix of the deceased author appointed by the court after the Executor(s) or Executrix (death)
NK	Next of kin of deceased author (other than surviving spouse or children)
PCB	Proprietor of copyright in a work copyrighted by a corporate body other than as assignee or licensee of the individual author
PCW	Proprietor of copyright in a composite work
PPW	Proprietor of copyright in a posthumous work
PWH	Proprietor of copyright in a work made for hire
W	Widow of the author
Wr	Widower of the author

Other Helpful Materials

Related Files
DIALOG TRADEMARKSCAN® files available online
• Brands and Their Companies File 116
• TRADEMARKSCAN® – U.S. FEDERAL File 226

• TRADEMARKSCAN® – U.S. STATE File 246
• BEGIN TRADEMKS gives access to all.
• DATASTAR IMSMARQ gateway to 12 trademark files.

Other Search Aids	
ONLINE on DIALOG	HELP RATES 120 HELP FMT 120 (for pre- defined format options)

ASAF – Call 800-496-4470 or 415-254-8246 to place an order for the following FREE documents:	
Document	**ASAF #**
U.S. Copyrights Bluesheet	120

WWW SITES
www.dialog.com
U.S. Copyright Office – Publication Information, call 202-707-3000. Information & Reference Division, (202-707-6850) for a search report.

FEDERAL REGISTER

Searching for Titles and Parts of the Code of Federal Regulations in DIALOG File 669

File 669, **Federal Register**, provides the full text of the daily *Federal Register* publication, starting from January 1988 to the present. The *Federal Register* is the official publication of the U.S. federal government, published with the purpose of notifying the public of official agency actions. This is the medium used to communicate regulations and legal notices published by Federal Agencies. The Code of Federal Regulations (CFR) is an annually revised codification of the rules that have been published in the *Federal Register*. The CFR is divided into 50 titles related to different agencies or topical areas. FARS (Federal Acquisition Regulations) is Title 48 of the CFR.

This document contains:

• A search example of how to search for a specific title and part of the Code of Federal Regulations

- Answers to frequently asked questions on the Federal Register and on search features of File 669.

Searching for a Specific Title and Part of the Code of Federal Regulations

Let's assume that you were assigned to find anything published in the *Federal Register* on a given date, April 8, 1996, regarding Title 29, Part 1904 (Recording and Reporting Occupational Injuries and Illnesses) of the Code of Federal Regulations. A recommended strategy for retrieving this record is as follows:

Command Summary

B	669
S	29()CFR(S)1904/CF
S	S1 AND PD=(960408 OR APRIL 08, 1996)
T	S2/8
T	S2/9

Search Strategy

?b 669	BEGIN File 669.
? s 29(w)cfr(s)1904/cf	SELECT the title and part of the Code of Federal Regulations, using the /CF suffix to restrict retrieval to the CFR Sections Affected field. This prevents possible retrieval from a Table of Contents record.

```
      1433   29/CF
     72923   CFR/CF
        10   1904/CF
S1       8   29()CFR(S)1904/CF
```

? s s1 and pd=(960408 or april 08, 1996)	Combine the previous set with the Publication Date field entry for April 8, 1996, using the PD= search prefix.

```
        8   S1
      168   PD=960408
      168   PD=APRIL 08, 1996
  S2     1  S1 AND PD=(960408 OR APRIL 08, 1996)
```

? t s2/8	TYPE the record in Format 8 to determine article length. For pricing information, enter HELP RATES 669.

2/8/1

DIALOG(R)File 669:(c) 1996 Knight-Ridder Info. All rts. reserv.

00579332

Recording and Reporting Occupational Injuries and Illnesses; Notice of Meeting; Extension of Comment Period

WORD COUNT: 69

?t s2/9	As this is a fairly short article, TYPE this article in Format 9, full format.

2/9/1

DIALOG(R)File 669:Federal Register

(c) 1996 Knight-Ridder Info. All rts. reserv.

00579332

Recording and Reporting Occupational Injuries and Illnesses; Notice of Meeting; Extension of Comment Period

                         Vol. 61, No. 068

                         61 FR 15435

                         Monday, April 08, 1996

AGENCY: DEPARTMENT OF LABOR (DOL); Occupational Safety and Health Administration (OSHA)

DOC TYPE: Proposed Rules

CFR: 29 CFR Parts 1904 and 1952

DATES: The public meeting will be held April 30, 1996 beginning at 8:30 a.m. and extend through May 1, if necessary. Persons wishing to make presentations should contact Tom Hall on or before April 19, 1996. OSHA invites the public to submit written comments on the NPRM on or before May 31, 1996.

CONTACT: FOR FURTHER INFORMATION CONTACT: Ms. Anne Cyr, U.S. Department of Labor, OSHA, Room N-3647, 200 Constitution Avenue NW., Washington, DC 20210, (202) 219-8148.

ADDRESSES: The meeting will be held at the U.S. Department of Labor, 200 Constitution Avenue NW., Washington, DC 20210 in Room S-4215. Persons wishing to make presentations should contact Tom Hall at U.S. Department of Labor, OSHA, Room N-3647, 200 Constitution Avenue NW, Washington D.C. 20210, (202) 219-8148. Written comments are to be submitted in writing in quadruplicate to: Docket Officer, Docket No. R-02, Occupational Safety and

Health Administration, Room N- 2625, U.S. Department of Labor , 200 Constitution Avenue NW, Washington D.C. 20210, telephone (202) 219-7894.

ACTION: Proposed rule; notice of meeting.

SUMMARY: OSHA published a Notice of Proposed Rulemaking covering the recording and reporting of workplace deaths, injuries and illnesses, which appeared in the Federal Register on February 2, 1996 (61 FR 4030). OSHA held a public meeting regarding this proposal from March 26 to March 29, 1996. In response to a request from other interested stakeholders who were unable to attend this meeting, OSHA will hold an additional public meeting beginning on April 30, 1996. The purpose of the meeting is to give the public another opportunity to provide information to OSHA concerning issues

raised by the proposal. As a result of the scheduling
of this second public meeting, OSHA is extending the
end of the public comment period from May 2 to May 31,
1996.

WORD COUNT: 69

TEXT:

SUPPLEMENTARY INFORMATION: The meeting will be open
to the public. Seating, however, is limited and will
 be available on a first-come, first-serve basis.
The amount of time available for each presenter may be
limited by OSHA, if necessary.

    Signed in Washington, D.C., this 3rd day of April,
1996.

Joseph A. Dear,

Assistant Secretary of Labor.

INTERNAL DATA: FR Doc. 96-8674; Filed 4-5-96; 8:45 am;
BILLING CODE 4510-26-P

NOTE:

If you do not use a Basic Index field suffix,
e.g., /AG for Agency, you will be searching all
Basic Index fields.

If you are searching the entire Basic Index,
and do not want to retrieve Table of Contents
records, be sure to NOT out Table of Contents
records using the DT= prefix, e.g., **SELECT
S1 NOT DT=TABLE ?**

Never TYPE an article without first **TYPE**ing it
first in Format 8 to determine the length of the
article, e.g., TYPE S2/8/ALL.

FREQUENTLY ASKED QUESTIONS

Where can old data for the Federal Register be found?

* File 669 only goes back to January 1988. For older data, there are
  abstracts and indexing available in File 136 going back to 1977.

> ## What do the header numbers mean at the beginning of each record?

Each record in File 669 contains a header in the following format:

Vol. 61, No. 103	This is the Volume and Number.
61 FR 25135	This is the Official Citation.
Monday, May 28, 1996	The day of the week and calendar date.

- The Volume Number identifies the year of publication. Thus Vol. 61 is 1996, Vol. 60 is 1995,Vol. 53 is 1988. The Number (No. 103) identifies the issue, or day or publication. The number will increase by 1 for each workday, there being approximately 250 workdays per year. Therefore, No. 001 is the first workday in January, and No. 250 would be near the end of December.

- The Official Citation indicates the Volume (61) of the *Federal Register* (FR) and the page number (25135) where the article begins.

- Calendar dates are searchable using the PD= field. It is recommended that you search for dates both as a phrase using the name of the month, day, command, year (e.g., SELECT PD=MAY 28, 1996), and in the format YYMMDD, where YY represents the year, MM the month, and DD the day (e.g., SELECT PD=960528). Put these two dates in the same SELECT statement, e.g., SELECT PD=(MAY 28, 1996 OR 960528).

> ## How do I find a document using the official citation?

- A field for the official citation was added in February 1990 and is searchable using /CI or CI=. A citation can be searched using either word or phrase indexing, e.g., SELECT CI=55 FR 15150 or SELECT 55()FR()15150/CI or SELECT (55(S)15150)/CI.

> ## How can I find information on the CFR section affected?

- Use the /CF field suffix with the title and section(s) affected. The subsections may not be included. For example, to find information affecting Title 21 (Food and Drugs) Section 558, SELECT 21()CFR(S)558/CF. Do NOT enter numbers as ranges, since this field is not numerically indexed.

How can I find information using the page number?

- A field for the page number was added in February 1990 and is searchable using the PG= prefix. The page number can be ANDed to the year or publication date, i.G., SELECT PG=38816 AND PY=1993 or SELECT PG=38816 AND PD=930720. Only the starting page of the article is indexed and searchable. It is not possible to access individual pages of a Federal Register article.

How can the Table of Contents for the Federal Register be called up?

- There is a Document Type field that can be used to pull up Table of Contents records using SELECT DT=TABLE ? This can be ANDed to a publication date, e.g., SELECT DT=TABLE ? AND PD=960429.

How do I know in advance if there are extremely long records in my set?

- Type the information first in Format 8, which gives the word count, title, and DIALOG Accession Number. As a rule of thumb, 400 to 500 words will fill one 8.5-in. by 11-in. sheet of paper, single-spaced. Order very long records with the PRINT command, e.g., PRINT S1/9/ALL or using the DIALOG Accession Number, PRINT 00511685/9.

KWIC (Key Word In Context) isn't working. What's wrong?

- The KWIC window can accommodate up to 32,000 words. Many records in the Federal Register are longer than 32,000 words, so KWIC will not work in these records. For pricing information, enter HELP RATES 669.

Are there Wage Scales in the Federal Register?

- No, actual wage or salary scales are not included in the Federal Register. Please contact your nearest Federal Building, Personnel Department. The Federal Register does contain changes in rules or regulations for determining salaries, such as changes in rules for overtime pay.

Other Helpful Materials

Related Files
DIALOG
PAIS INTERNATIONAL File 49

GPO MONTHLY CATALOG File 66
U.S. POLITICAL SCIENCE DOCUMENTS File 93
ASI (AMERICAN STATISTICS INDEX) File 102
CONGRESSIONAL RECORD ABSTRACTS File 135
FEDERAL REGISTER ABSTRACTS File 136
WASHINGTON POST ONLINE File 146
GPO PUBLICATIONS REFERENCE FILE File 166
BNA DAILY NEWS FROM WASHINGTON File 655
FEDERAL NEWS SERVICE File 660
Other Search Aids
ONLINE on DIALOG
HELP RATES 669
HELP FMT 669 (for pre-defined format options)
HELP LIMIT 669
HELP FIELD 669
ASAF--Call 800-496-4470 or 415-254-8246 to place an order for the following FREE documents:
Document ASAF #
FEDERAL REGISTER Bluesheet 3669

INDEX

D

R

research
  copyright searches
    medium used for material, 126
    name of author, 126
    name of work, 126
  copyright searches, 126
  defining the scope, 124
  Internet, 130
    intellectual property searches, 133
  manual design mark search, 128
  manual research, 128
    copyright registration search, 129
    early patent and papers, 128
    search for common law trademark use, 129
    university research, 128
  online searching, 126
    dangers of incompleteness, 129
  paralegal responsibility, 124
  patent searches, 124
    area of invention, 124
    common industry terms, 124
  requirement for, 123
  search firms, 124
  trademark searches
    length and size of marks, 125
    meaning of mark, 125
    phonetics of mark, 125
    proposed use of mark, 125
    variations of mark, 126
  trademark searches, 125
Restatement of Torts, 106, 107, 108
RHODE ISLAND RED®, 36
right of publicity, 109, 110
  private individuals, 111
  public figures, 110
Robeson, Abigail, 111
Rochester Folding Box Company, 112
Roe v. Wade, 110

S

Samsung, 111
semiconductor chip protection, xiii

service marks
  defined, 35, 36
Snow White, 125
Sony, 41
Sony v. Betamax, 80
Spandex®, 4
suggestive marks, 39
Supplemental Register, 45, 51, 56, 60

T

Taylor, Elizabeth, 111
Texas Instruments, 2
Thomson & Thomson, 124, 134, 217
trade names, 36
trade secrets, xiii, 105
  business information, 107
  competitive advantage of idea, 109
  court protection, 107
  defined, 107
  economic considerations, 105
  improper disclosure, 106
  information classified as secret, 106
  Internet, 108
  principles, 106
trademark applications
  abandonment, 55
  actual use applications, 49
  amendments to allege use, 56, 57
  appeals, 56
  applications based on foreign registration, 57
  applications based on foreign registrations, 50
  appointment of domestic representative, 53
  bases, 47
  concurrent use appliations, 50
  drawing sheet, 53
  elements, 47, 48
  filing dates, 48
  final office actions, 55
  initial deadlines, 54
  intent-to-use applications, 49, 58
  international applications
    foreign associates, 68
    initial deadlines, 68
    license agreements, 69

U